FAIRFIELD HIGH
SCHOOL LIBRARY

Critical Thinking About
Environmental Issues

Forest Fires

Other books in the Critical Thinking About
Environmental Issues series include:

Endangered Species
Energy
Global Warming
Pesticides

Critical Thinking About
Environmental Issues

Forest Fires

by Linda E. Platts

Jane S. Shaw, *Series Editor*
Senior Associate
PERC, The Center for Free
Market Environmentalism

GREENHAVEN
PRESS®

San Diego • Detroit • New York • San Francisco • Cleveland
New Haven, Conn. • Waterville, Maine • London • Munich

© 2004 by Greenhaven Press. Greenhaven Press is an imprint of The Gale Group, Inc., a division of Thomson Learning, Inc.

Greenhaven® and Thomson Learning™ are trademarks used herein under license.

For more information, contact
Greenhaven Press
27500 Drake Rd.
Farmington Hills, MI 48331-3535
Or you can visit our Internet site at http://www.gale.com

ALL RIGHTS RESERVED.
No part of this work covered by the copyright hereon may be reproduced or used in any form or by any means—graphic, electronic, or mechanical, including photocopying, recording, taping, Web distribution or information storage retrieval systems—without the written permission of the publisher.

LIBRARY OF CONGRESS CATALOGING-IN-PUBLICATION DATA

Platts, Linda E.
  Forest fires / by Linda E. Platts
    v. cm. — (Critical thinking about environmental issues)
  Includes bibliographical references and index.
  Summary: Examines the role that forest fires have played throughout history, the way forests are managed, the effectiveness of firefighting, and future concerns.
    ISBN 0-7377-2300-9 (hardback: alk. paper)
    1. Forest fires—Juvenile literature. 2. Forest fires—Prevention and control—Juvenile literature [1. Forest fires.] I. Title. II. Critical thinking about environmental issues series.
    SD421.23.P53 2004
    634.9'618—dc22
                                                                     2003016051

Printed in the United States of America

Contents

Foreword	6
Introduction	8

Chapter 1
Forest Fires: Something New?   10

Chapter 2
How Should Forests Be Managed?   22

Chapter 3
Should Fires Be Fought?   38

Chapter 4
The Bitterroot Fires: A Case Study   50

Chapter 5
What Comes Next?   63

Notes	77
Glossary	81
For Further Reading	83
Works Consulted	84
Acknowledgments	90
Index	91
Picture Credits	96
About the Author	96

Foreword

> If a nation expects to be ignorant and free ... it expects what never was and never will be.
>
> Thomas Jefferson

Thomas Jefferson understood that a free nation depends on an educated citizenry. Citizens must have the level of knowledge necessary to make informed decisions on complex public policy issues. In the United States, schools have a major responsibility for developing that knowledge.

In the twenty-first century, American citizens will struggle with environmental questions of the first order. These include complicated and contentious topics such as global warming, pesticide use, and species extinction. The goal of this series, Critical Thinking About Environmental Issues, is to help young people recognize the complexity of these topics and help them view the issues analytically and objectively.

All too often, environmental problems are treated as moral issues. For example, using pesticides is often considered bad because residues may be found on food and because the application of pesticides may harm birds. In contrast, relying on organic food (produced without insecticides or herbicides) is considered good. Yet this simplistic approach fails to recognize the role of pesticides in producing food for the world and ignores the scientific studies that suggest that pesticides cause little harm to humans. Such superficial treatment of multifaceted issues does not serve citizens well and provides a poor basis for education.

This series, Critical Thinking About Environmental Issues, exposes students to the complexities of each issue it addresses. While the books touch on many aspects of each environmental problem, their goal is primarily to point out the differences in scientific opinion surrounding the topics. These books present the facts that underlie different scientific interpretations. They also address differing values that may affect the interpretation of the facts and economic questions that may affect policy choices.

The goal of the series is to open up inquiry on issues that are often viewed too narrowly. Each book, written in language that is understandable to young readers, provides enough information about the scientific theories and methods for the reader to weigh the merits of the leading arguments. Ultimately, students, like adult citizens, will make their own decisions.

With environmental issues, especially those where new science is always emerging, the possibility exists that there is not enough information to settle the issue. If this is the case, the books may spur readers to pursue the topics further. If readers come away from this series critically examining their own opinions as well as others' and eager to seek more information, the goal of these books will have been achieved.

by Jane S. Shaw
Series Editor

INTRODUCTION

For decades Americans have battled forest fires believing that they were saving valuable living landscapes from certain destruction. Yet where fire has been eliminated, forest health has suffered. Today scientists as well as government officials believe that the nation is facing a crisis in forest health.

Fires burned in North America for thousands of years before European settlers arrived. The fires were caused by lightning as well as by native peoples. As the country was settled, people grew increasingly fearful of the huge fires that burned valuable timber and millions of acres of land. The government made firefighting

A Colorado forest fire threatens a rural home. Although fires pose a tremendous threat to personal property, they are vital to the health of forests.

a high priority for all of the agencies that manage federal lands. The Forest Service as part of the Department of Agriculture fights fires on 190 million acres of national forest as well as adjacent lands where the fires spread, and the National Park Service, the Fish and Wildlife Service, and the Bureau of Land Management, all part of the Department of the Interior, fight fires on the millions of acres of land under their care.

As Americans became more proficient at putting out fires, science discovered the importance of fire to forest ecosystems. Many American forests actually depend on fire to help germinate seeds, remove competing trees, recycle nutrients, and provide habitat and nourishing food to wildlife. Science continues to provide new information about the complex relationship between fire and living things, but it cannot tell us how best to put this knowledge to work in the forest. Reintroducing fire to the landscape is essential to forest health. How this will be accomplished will be determined by politics and economics.

The world today is much different than when fires burned freely across the landscape and mountain valleys were filled with smoke for most of the summer. Millions of people inhabit these forested regions, and huge wildfires would threaten their lives, health, and property. Although some people recommend letting fires burn in remote areas but not near the edge of the forest where people live, others want the forest to be logged and thinned before any fires are allowed to burn. The question of how much it would cost and who would pay for it is also critical because the costs could be staggering.

The problems are complex, and the answers are difficult to discern.

CHAPTER 1

Forest Fires: Something New?

In June 1988 summer tourists flooded into Yellowstone National Park eager to see the Old Faithful geyser, fish the lakes and streams, and watch the grazing herds of elk and bison. The weather was unusually warm and dry that year, and several small fires started by lightning were already burning in the park. By July the worst drought in park history had taken hold. Meadows turned brown under the blazing sun and forests were parched for lack of moisture.

Without warning the warm breezes grew into strong winds, then into gales gusting up to eighty miles per hour, whipping small fires into a giant conflagration. Walls of flame two hundred feet high devoured the dry timber, and smoke rose in mushroom clouds to forty thousand feet.

The fires burned throughout the summer, finally closing in on Old Faithful at the end of August. "The afternoon turned black and the howling wind sounded like a jet engine,"[1] wrote reporter Rocky Barker. Those remaining at Old Faithful fled to the parking lot while hot coals branded their backs and burning embers flew past their heads. As the fire crested the surrounding hills and hurtled down upon them, fire crews raced to keep the flames at bay.

At one point ninety-five hundred firefighters battled the flames, including army and marine troops. They cleared firebreaks, dumped slurry from planes, sprayed fire retardant foam, and labored with hand tools to snuff out ground fires and clear away dry needles and branches. On August 20, in just a twenty-four-hour span, the flames consumed 165,000 acres. "We couldn't hold any of the fire lines,"[2] said Don Sholly, Yellowstone's chief ranger. Then, on September 11, a light snow fell, followed by cool, moist fall weather. The fire slowed, and the worst was over. By November winter had settled over the park, and the last of the fires was finally extinguished. Mother Nature had done the work that thousands of firefighters could not.

The enormity of the fire stunned park officials as well as research scientists. Eight hundred thousand acres, more than one-third of

Facilitated by drought and strong winds, flames race through a forest in Yellowstone National Park during the summer of 1988.

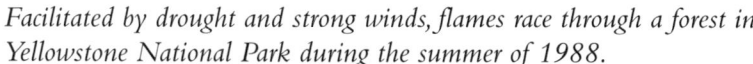

the 2.2-million-acre park, had been scorched, and another 800,000 acres had burned in adjoining forests. Since the park's founding in 1872, its largest fire had burned only 25,000 acres. The park's fire expert for sixteen years, Don Despain, had never seen any fire larger than 7,400 acres. "We were seeing things the fire experts had never experienced,"[3] said John Varley, Yellowstone's director of research.

The Debate over Fire

The Yellowstone fires sparked a debate that continues today, a debate that was rekindled in 1994 and 1996 and then again in 2000 and 2002, when even larger fires raged through western states during hot, dry summers. At issue is whether vast conflagrations like those at Yellowstone—unparalleled in most people's memory—represent natural events, something people should expect and prepare for, or whether they are the result of mistaken forest management policies that ought to be changed.

In the immediate aftermath of the fires, many people expressed anger and recriminations. Western politicians were outraged because they thought the blackened and charred forests would drive away tourists who brought needed income to their states. Their constituents clamored for help to replant the forests, to pay for more fire protection, and for assurances that such fires would never burn again. Some people claimed the fires had killed huge numbers of wild animals, destroyed wildlife habitat, and sterilized soils so that plants could not grow. They mourned the loss of majestic landscapes and were frightened by the threat the fires posed to their lives, health, and property.

[Some people] believed the forests had been in desperate need of fire to clean out the dead and diseased trees.

On the other side of the debate were those who welcomed the fires as a long overdue act of nature. They believed the forests had been in desperate need of fire to clean out the dead and diseased trees and create grassy meadows rich with forage for wildlife amid the dense growth. They argued that the unsightly ash covering the landscape contained rich deposits of minerals that would ensure the health of a new generation of trees and provide wildlife with nutritious grasses and shrubs. Although some animals had lost their homes, they saw evidence that other species had found new homes in the burned tree trunks and sunny forest openings. Carree Barkley, an extension forestry associate at the University of Idaho, has seen many forest fires and the blackened landscapes they leave behind. In her view, it is just another stage of the forest: "It will be incredible. It will be green. It will come back."[4]

Emotional reactions eventually gave way to more sobered analysis. Beginning in the early 1900s, American forest policy was to prevent forest fires at all costs. Yet research had indicated that fire was part of how a forest stayed healthy. Had suppressing fires been a mistake? Should forest fires have been allowed to burn? This topic elicited further investigation after the Yellowstone fires. To find the answers, many looked to the past.

Fires in the Past

Fires have burned in North America for millions of years. Scientists know this by studying the sediments that build up at the bottom of lakes and ponds. Charcoal and plant parts such as pollen, needles, and twigs are swept into the water. The charcoal is evidence of past fires and can tell scientists when fires burned and how often.

Scientists believe that lightning caused nearly all of the fires in ancient forests, but people changed that. When humans arrived in North America about twelve thousand years ago, they brought fire with them, often carrying live embers wrapped in leaves and bark to start their campfires. Some historians theorize that fire was so critical to survival that it was never deliberately extinguished. Even when groups moved on to a new location, they would leave their campfires burning.

Although early North Americans sometimes started fires unintentionally, they also set fires deliberately to help improve their food supplies. They cleared land for crops by burning the forests, and with more open land, they were able to spot game from long distances. They also burned areas close to their camps to attract

A family battles a wildfire in the late nineteenth century. By the early 1900s, American forest policy was designed to prevent all forest fires.

wildlife. These areas regrew with lush grasses and tender shrubs, enriched by the minerals from the fire's ashes.

In addition, North American Indians used flames to drive herds of grazing animals in a particular direction. In the West, they drove bison off cliffs to their deaths and then harvested the meat. Along the eastern seaboard, with its many bays and inlets, Indians used fire to drive the game onto narrow peninsulas, where they could be easily killed.

When European explorers sailed along the coast from Virginia to Florida, they were amazed by the pall of thick smoke that lay over the land. Italian navigator Giovanni da Verrazano noted in 1524 that the coastal plains were alight with large fires. Europeans saw these as remarkable because forest fires were almost unknown in Europe.

When Verrazano and his men marched inland through what would become Rhode Island, he reported finding open plains seventy-five to ninety miles long "entirely free from trees or other hindrances."[5] Fires had created the open plains and also kept the trees from regrowing. "The Americas as first seen by Europeans were not as they had been crafted by God, but as they had been created by native peoples,"[6] writes Charles Kay, a political scientist at Utah State University who has studied aboriginal life.

Human Fires Versus Natural Fires

Scientists have concluded that human-caused fires gradually produced changes in the landscape that were different than those resulting from natural fires. Once humans began setting fires, they began to change the nature and composition of the forest.

Natural fires, caused primarily by lightning, depend on the season, moisture, winds, and available fuels. Humans, on the other hand, can start a fire almost anywhere at any time.

In the West, dry lightning storms occur frequently during the summer; thus, most natural fires are summer fires. Before humans had much impact on North America, plants and animals adapted to this pattern of summer fires followed by regrowth. Plants would return to the burned area in a generally predictable way, known as succession. The first species to establish themselves were called pioneer species, and they in turn would be followed by other plants, each one preparing the stage for the next.

In contrast, Indians set fires in the late fall at the end of the growing season. By removing the underbrush, fallen trees, and low-hanging branches from the forest, they could travel and hunt more easily. Burning in the fall ensured that the fires would never burn too long or too far because the winter snows would eventually snuff them out.

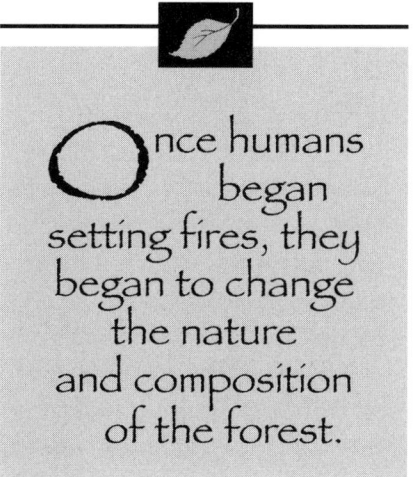

Once humans began setting fires, they began to change the nature and composition of the forest.

In the spring, Indians often burned again after the first snowmelt but before the new growth began. These fires also cleared debris and created openings in the forest that attracted wildlife and spurred the growth of grasses and other forage for game. When lightning-caused fires returned in the summer, there was less fuel in the forest. What might otherwise have been intense fires now burned more lightly. This addition of human-set fires to those caused by lightning changed not only the way fires burned but also the type of vegetation that grew.

In the Pacific Northwest, for example, the ancient forests of Engelmann spruce, mountain hemlock, and lodgepole pine that had grown after the last ice age were subject to massive burns by lightning as well as human-ignited fires. Douglas fir, which thrives in burned areas, moved in and replaced the earlier forests.

When Europeans arrived in the Northwest, they saw magnificent forests of towering Pacific Douglas fir. They believed these to be old-growth forests, but in reality, they were seeing forests created by both man and nature, not the ancient forests. "There certainly was no 'forest primeval'; in fact, 'old-growth' forests, as we know them today, were very rare in pre-Columbian times,"[7] writes Charles Kay.

Fires During Colonization

As European settlement expanded in the eastern portions of the country, native peoples were gradually pushed off the land. Free-ranging wildfires became less frequent during the 1600s and 1700s as settlers built permanent homes and villages. Unlike the Indians, whose nomadic lifestyle allowed them to move easily if wildfires burned too close to their camps, the new settlers were rooted to one location, and they discouraged fires near their towns and homesteads. The treeless plains and savannas, which had been created by fire, began to fill in with new forests.

In the West, however, free-ranging fires continued to burn. As they explored the continent in the early 1800s, Meriwether Lewis and William Clark reported seeing Indians setting fire to the prairie to drive bison. As late as 1889 John Wesley Powell, then director of the U.S. Geological Survey, described a smoky train trip from the Dakotas west through the Rocky Mountains. "Among the valleys, with mountains on every side, during all that trip a mountain was never seen. This was because the fires in the mountains created such smoke that the whole country was enveloped by it and hidden from view."[8]

Western settlers helped create those fires. Indeed, Powell's train may have contributed to them. Four railroads now crisscrossed the continent, and wood-burning locomotives continually spewed hot embers from their smokestacks, sometimes setting fire to the landscape on either side of the tracks. Trains became one of the major causes of fire as they moved through the arid western landscape during the summer months. Other sources of fire were the commonly used woodstoves. Sparks from a stove could easily set wood shingles on fire, and in a dry season the fire could engulf a whole community and spread into nearby forests. The settlers also continued to use fire to improve grazing for livestock and clear land for crops. According to Roger A. Sedjo, who directs the Forest Economics and Policy Program for the Washington, D.C., research organization Resources for the Future, the settlers "viewed the century-old trees as impediments to agricultural development."[9]

"Timber Famine"

By the late 1800s the fires that were once considered as much a part of the western landscape as the forests came to be viewed as a threat—to both the growing population and the nation's timber supply. These concerns forced major changes in government policies toward fire and forest protection.

The nation's supply of trees had once appeared limitless, but people began to worry about running out of wood, especially since more people were using wood. The country's population jumped from 5.8 million to 76 million between 1800 and 1900. By 1920 another 30 million had been added, bringing the total to 106 million Americans.

People continued to cut down the forests to make land available for agriculture, and at the same time the country was entering an industrial age. Wood was widely used to fuel smelters, steamboats, and trains and to heat homes and businesses. Wood was the most common construction material used in buildings, roads, railroads, fences, mines, and bridges. American forests fueled the growth of the nation.

To meet the demand, logging expanded from the East to the Great Lakes states and into the South. The massive demand created a virtual free-for-all in the forests. Much of the timber was on public land, but the laws that governed the use and ownership of the land were meant to help small farmers establish homesteads. There were no provisions for the sale of trees or timber production. Often, trespassers harvested the timber and moved on because they owned neither the land nor the timber. They used poor harvesting techniques, removing the largest and healthiest trees while leaving behind huge piles of slash and debris, and they certainly did no replanting. "Effectively the forest belonged to no one; thus the timber was there for the taking,"[10] Sedjo writes.

By the end of the nineteenth century, many of the great forests of the East, Midwest, and South had been ravaged by logging. It was assumed that western forests would be next unless the cutting was controlled or stopped. A growing conservation movement, combined with fear of a possible "timber famine," spurred Congress to pass the Forest Reserve Act in 1891. It authorized the president to set aside public land as reserves for the future, where timber harvesting was not allowed. Eventually these reserves became the national forests.

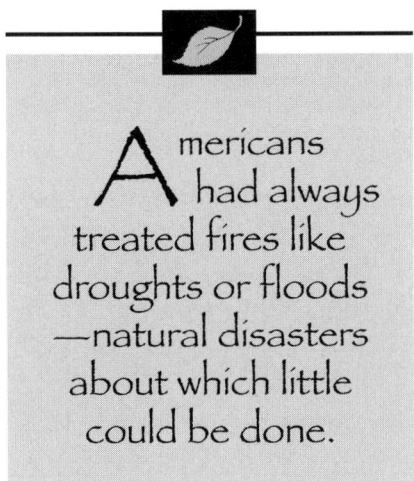

Americans had always treated fires like droughts or floods—natural disasters about which little could be done.

Although timber harvesting was halted on the reserves, fires continued to burn unabated. Americans had always treated fires like droughts or floods—natural disasters about which little could be done. The concept of putting out forest fires was relatively new. The American public was just beginning to see fire as a destructive force that could be controlled. The crusade against fire grew in part from the public's interest in protecting the forests.

In 1905 the Forest Service was founded to protect America's forest resources. Fire control and prevention were the young agency's top priorities. In 1908, Congress provided special funding to the Forest Service to fight forest fires. No restrictions were placed on the amount of money that could be used because no one could predict how much would be needed.

Logs are stacked outside a Minnesota sawmill. By the early twentieth century, the logging industry had ravaged forests in the Midwest, East, and South.

The agency's early confidence that it could control fires was dashed in August 1910, when a firestorm fanned by hurricane-force winds burned 3 million acres of Idaho, Montana, and Washington, killing eighty-five people in just two days. More legislation followed to assist forest firefighting and coordinate efforts between local, state, and federal agencies in the form of the Weeks Act of 1911 and the Clark-McNary Act of 1924. In the coming years, the Forest Service would learn to battle fire with the same intensity and dedication with which the armed forces went to war.

Preventing Forest Fires

In addition to battling fires, the Forest Service focused on fire prevention. In 1944 it launched one of the most successful advertising campaigns of all time. A couple of cartoon characters led the way, encouraging the public to prevent fires in the forests.

Walt Disney's 1944 movie *Bambi* featured a motherless fawn; Bambi soon became the first symbol for the Forest Service's fire prevention campaign. Anyone who has seen the movie will remember the poignant scene of a terrified Bambi fleeing from the forest fire as flames lapped at his heels. Disney agreed to lend the use of Bambi's image to the Forest Service for one year, and the vulnerable little fawn succeeded in riveting public attention on the danger of forest fires and the role that ordinary people could play in preventing them.

Following the success of Bambi, the Forest Service adopted its own icon, Smokey Bear. Smokey made his debut on a 1944

In 1944 the Forest Service introduced Smokey Bear as part of its campaign to encourage the American public to prevent forest fires.

poster dousing a campfire with a bucket of water. His message, "Remember—Only *you* can PREVENT FOREST FIRES!"[11] soon became part of American culture. Typically dressed in a broad-brimmed forest ranger's hat and a pair of blue jeans, Smokey was adored by children and adults alike. In 1952 an act of Congress took Smokey out of the public domain and placed him under the control of the Department of Agriculture.

Smokey remains a popular figure with children today, but his message has been updated and targeted to adults. Smokey is still reminding Americans to put out campfires and crush cigarettes, but his message has changed. He tells Americans to prevent wildfires, not forest fires. By wildfires, he means fires accidentally set by people. Today many experts agree that fires—forest fires—are a natural part of many forest systems in North America. By ignoring the history of fire on this continent, a growing number of people believe the nation took a wrong turn when it attempted to suppress all fires.

Meanwhile, wildland firefighting, which was virtually unheard-of in the 1800s, has become a profession employing thousands of people and the most advanced technology. Some firefighters work year-round, but most of them are on duty only during the summer fire season, when they are part of some of the largest mobilizations of manpower and equipment outside of an actual war. In addition to smoke jumpers and others battling the blazes directly, there are equipment manufacturers, caterers, transportation companies, fuel suppliers, refuse companies, and a host of other specialized services geared to firefighting.

Conclusion

Scientific evidence and early written histories point to fire's pervasive effect on the American landscape. After nearly one hundred years of fire suppression, the Forest Service is questioning its policy of putting out all fires. Beginning in 1988 with the fires in Yellowstone National Park, major forest fires in the West have forced many people to reexamine the issue of fire in our forests. Should humankind take a more active part in managing forest fires? Or should humans accept them as a natural occurrence and let them burn? The questions are many, and answers are still sketchy.

CHAPTER 2

How Should Forests Be Managed?

On a warm spring day in Montana's Bitterroot National Forest, a plume of white smoke rises from a ridge and drifts slowly across the valley below. Firefighters working for the Forest Service move carefully through the woods with drip torches, a tool that spews ignited liquid fuel onto the ground. Their job is to set the forest on fire. For these disciples of Smokey Bear, setting fires once would have been an unthinkable act. Now scientists have a better understanding of fire's role in the forest and know that it is vital to a healthy forest.

For nearly a century, however, the Forest Service put out fires that it mistakenly believed were damaging to the forests. The agency extinguished fires—started by both lightning and humans—that had historically burned across the American landscape. During this same period, forest health spiraled downward.

Fires and Forest Health

The logical question is why did the Forest Service put out fires if, in fact, fire is critical to healthy forests? The answer is that it took scientists many decades to understand the connection between fire and forest health, and as research continues, more is learned. Indians understood that fire was a useful tool in the forest; early settlers also observed benefits from fire. Today, strong scientific evidence, not just observations, confirms the beneficial relationship of fire to forest ecosystems. After thousands of years of coexistence with fire, many forests are not just adapted to fire but require fire. It performs a variety of essential functions, including germinating seeds, cycling nutrients, and creating a mosaic of open spaces to support a diversity of species. This study of relationships between organisms and their environment, known as ecology, is a young science. Discoveries are being made all the time that aid forest managers. For their part, managers must constantly adjust how they care for the forests as the understanding of forests improves.

Science, however, does not operate in a vacuum. For most of the twentieth century, the public supported fire suppression. A generation of Americans grew up with Smokey Bear warning of the danger of fire. Politicians were eager to support firefighting in order to save the forests and also please the voters at home. Changing deeply held beliefs that fire is the enemy of beautiful green forests has been a difficult undertaking.

Today the Forest Service sets fires, called prescribed burns, in areas that could benefit from burning to remove dense undergrowth or stop an insect infestation. Every effort is made to limit these fires to a specific area that has been determined in advance by the foresters. Occasionally these fires burn beyond their boundaries, growing too large for firefighters to control. They destroy homes, businesses, and even crops. It is because of fire's unpredictable nature that prescribed fires are set with the greatest caution.

Some lightning-caused fires also are allowed to burn under the careful watch of firefighters. These fires, too, are allowed to burn only in areas previously identified by foresters as being able to benefit from fire. Typically they are in remote areas and pose no threat to communities or private property.

Thousands of fires are ignited every year in the national forests as well as other forestland. Although a few fires are allowed to burn, the Forest Service continues to put out 99 percent of all fires. Its success has been notable, and the number of acres burned declined from the early 1900s until the last decades of the century, according to David Bunnell, recently retired from the Forest Service's Fire Use Program in Boise, Idaho. During the 1980s, the trend began to reverse. More acres are burning, and fires are returning to the forests despite aggressive firefighting.

There also is concern that the fires burning today are bigger and hotter than most fires of the past. An extended drought and warmer temperatures have contributed to the problem. Furthermore, the forests have been without fire for so long that poor health, a buildup of debris on the forest floor, and unnaturally dense conditions make them highly flammable. One hundred years ago ponderosa pine forests in the West typically had thirty to forty large trees to an acre because light-burning ground fires cleared out most of the young seedlings. Today those same forests have as many as one thousand to two thousand small-diameter trees crowded onto a single acre. This tremendous fuel load creates fires that many scientists believe are beyond the scope of what the forest can withstand. Uncertainty about how well the forest will recover from such huge fires coupled with concern for the public's health, safety, and property, make these fires unacceptable risks for the Forest Service.

The consensus among scientists, foresters, and the public is that "the Forest Service faces a forest health crisis of tremendous pro-

Firefighters set a controlled fire, or prescribed burn, in an Arizona forest. Prescribed burns help remove underbrush and stop insect infestations.

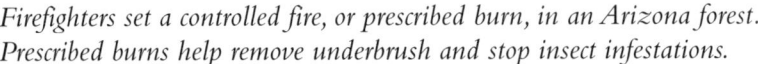

portions."[12] According to a government report, more than 70 million acres are at risk to fires so severe that they threaten both human safety and ecosystem integrity. Determining what to do about fire is the Forest Service's most difficult challenge.

Forest Service Professionals

Before tackling the problem of fires, it is helpful to understand more about the Forest Service, how it began and how it has changed. Over time the agency has supplied the nation with everything from timber and pure water to recreation, wildlife, and biodiversity. As public values have changed and science has advanced, the agency's goals have shifted in response. Even now, at the beginning of a new century, these goals and how to achieve them continue to be the subject of debate by the general public, environmental organizations, the timber industry, scientists, and forest managers.

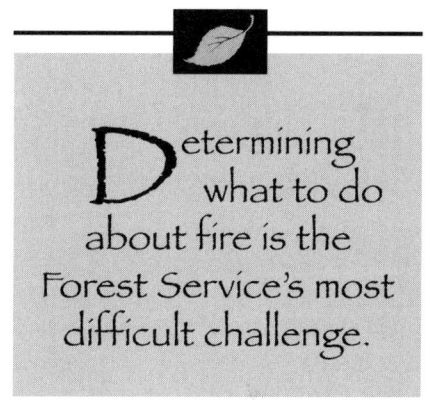

Determining what to do about fire is the Forest Service's most difficult challenge.

President Theodore Roosevelt founded the Forest Service in 1905. He was an avowed nature lover, but when it came to the national forests, he made it clear that he believed they should be put to practical use:

> The object is not to preserve the forests because they are beautiful, though that is good in itself, nor because they are refuges for the wild creatures of the wilderness, though that too is good in itself, but the primary goal of our forest policy ... is the making of prosperous homes ... a forest which contributes nothing to the wealth, progress or safety of the country is of no interest to the Government and should be of little interest to the forester.[13]

Roosevelt appointed Gifford Pinchot the first chief of the Forest Service. A Yale graduate who had studied forestry in Europe, he appeared the perfect choice to run an efficient and productive new agency. The Progressive Era was in full swing, and Americans were riding a wave of optimism. They were supremely confident that trained professionals such as Pinchot could solve any problem with scientific management. Several American universities had recently opened schools of forestry, and the ranks of the newly formed Forest Service were filled with eager young graduates.

Pinchot's ambition was to create forests that were as orderly and efficient as those in Europe. Yet European forests differed from their American counterparts in nearly every aspect, including tree species, soil, moisture, climate, topography, and fire frequency. Furthermore, Europe had already experienced a timber famine. Most of the continent's forests had been cut down. By the late 1800s European forests were being carefully managed to ensure a reliable source of timber by planting and harvesting on a regular rotation.

When Pinchot took charge of the Forest Service, many Americans feared a timber famine. Western lumbermen were carelessly razing vast swaths of forest, taking the largest, most valuable, and most fire-resistant trees, leaving behind piles of slash and debris. Pinchot wanted to eliminate such wasteful practices and apply the discipline of science to forest management. Like other progressives at the time, he believed it was possible to eliminate chaos and disorder from the natural forest and perfect it to serve human needs—to provide timber to build homes and improve lives.

Firefighting Takes Center Stage

Plans for order and efficiency in the forest were derailed by the "Big Blowup" of 1910 in Montana, Idaho, and Washington. In a summer of searing heat and unrelenting drought, eyewitnesses reported that smoke from the 3-million-acre fire darkened the skies as far east as New York State and was so thick to the west that ships five hundred miles at sea could not navigate by the stars. Some of the nation's finest white pine forests were lost, and by some estimates the dead timber could have filled a freight train twenty-four hundred miles long. Less than 10 percent of the timber was salvaged. In the aftermath of 1910, a public outcry against forest fires was heard across the nation. The fire had "managed to burn its way through public indifference,"[14] wrote Stewart Holbrook in his book on forest fires, *Burning an Empire*.

The devastation caused by the Big Blowup Fire of 1910 (timber salvaged from the fire is pictured) caused the Forest Service to focus its efforts on fighting fires.

From that point on, the Forest Service declared war on fire. Firefighting remains a top priority for the agency, supported by almost unlimited funds from Congress that now top $1.5 billion a year. Pinchot publicly supported the war on fire. "The work of a Forest Ranger is first of all to protect the district committed to his charge against fire. That comes before all else,"[15] he wrote. And William Greeley, who also served as chief of the Forest Service, pointed out that "firefighting is a matter of scientific management,"[16] so it clearly was a job suited for the Forest Service.

Although the professional foresters called for the elimination of fire, many who lived and worked in the forest viewed such plans as nothing less than absurd. In the Blue Mountains of eastern Washington and Oregon, Indians had frequently set fire to the forests. The Europeans who settled in the area learned the many benefits of fire firsthand and adopted the light-burning practices of the native tribes. However, the Forest Service's young professionals worshiped science and dismissed local expertise. This blind faith in scientific management had disastrous consequences for the forests at the end of the twentieth century. Robert H. Nelson, a professor of environmental policy at the University of Maryland, writes, "The most important forest fire lessons of the twentieth century were learned through practical experience and trial and error, not through formal research."[17]

In the years that followed, the Forest Service, working with other federal land management agencies, including the National Park Service and the Bureau of Land Management, built the most powerful firefighting force in the world. Fire towers were constructed, military planes were called into service, and firefighters were rigorously trained.

Is Fire the Villain?

Although the public strongly supported fire suppression (firefighting), as did many foresters and other scientists, some people questioned the policy. The evidence that fire was not always the villain was there for those who wanted to see it. Surprisingly, one of these was Gifford Pinchot. Despite his public stance against fire, in 1899 he wrote an article for *National Geographic* titled "The Relation of Forests and Forest Fires." Based on his experience in American forests, he discussed the importance of fire in clearing dense undergrowth and aiding in the reproduction of certain species. Yet he abruptly concluded his article, stating, "I hasten to add that these facts do not imply any desirability in the fires which are now devastating the West."[18] Although he had personally observed the benefits of fire, it conflicted with his vision of an orderly and efficient forest. Over the years other foresters also recognized the usefulness of fire, but few of them were able to stand against the tide of public and professional opinion that called for the eradication of fire. The second half of the twentieth century brought to light new evidence, and the case against fire began to unravel.

This unraveling began in part with the giant sequoia, one of the world's oldest and largest living organisms, which grows on the west slope of the Sierra Nevada mountains. The trees can live more than three thousand years and measure more than three hundred feet in height and thirty-five feet in diameter. These valuable trees were easy targets for early lumbermen. To protect the remaining groves of stately giants, Sequoia National Park was established in 1890.

How Should Forests Be Managed?

Even though the park provided protection from both lumbering and fire, by the 1960s park rangers were increasingly concerned about the giant sequoias in their care. The mature trees seemed healthy, but no new trees had taken root. Some of the youngest trees in the park were more than one hundred years old. At about the same time, the University of Arizona Laboratory of Tree-Ring Research provided some clues. By examining the fire scars on the growth rings, scientists assembled a fire history dating back two thousand years. Their research revealed that low- to moderate-intensity fires had burned in the groves as often as every three to eight years and that much hotter fires had burned less frequently. Obviously, the trees had lived successfully with fire for centuries.

Further research shed light on the relationship between the sequoias and fire. Fire not only caused the cones to release the seeds but also prepared the seed bed for the fledgling trees. To test these theories, several experimental burns were conducted on plots in

Giant sequoias like this one can live for thousands of years. During the 1960s, scientists discovered that wildfires promote the health of sequoia forests.

sequoia groves. The plot that burned the hottest produced more than forty thousand seedlings, whereas the plot with a lighter burn germinated about thirteen thousand seedlings. The control plot, which had no burning, did not produce a single seedling.

Responding to this discovery of the sequoia's dependence on fire, new policies that recognized the ecological importance of fire were established for both Sequoia and Kings Canyon National Parks. By the late 1960s fires started by lightning were allowed to burn, and prescribed fires were set in certain groves to promote new growth. The Forest Service eventually followed the lead of the Park Service, and beginning in the 1970s it allowed some fires to burn unhampered. The amount of land affected was small, but it represented a huge change in thinking by an agency dedicated to fighting fires.

The Environmental Movement

A profound shift in public attitudes was also taking place. Reverence for progress was replaced by reverence for nature. One of

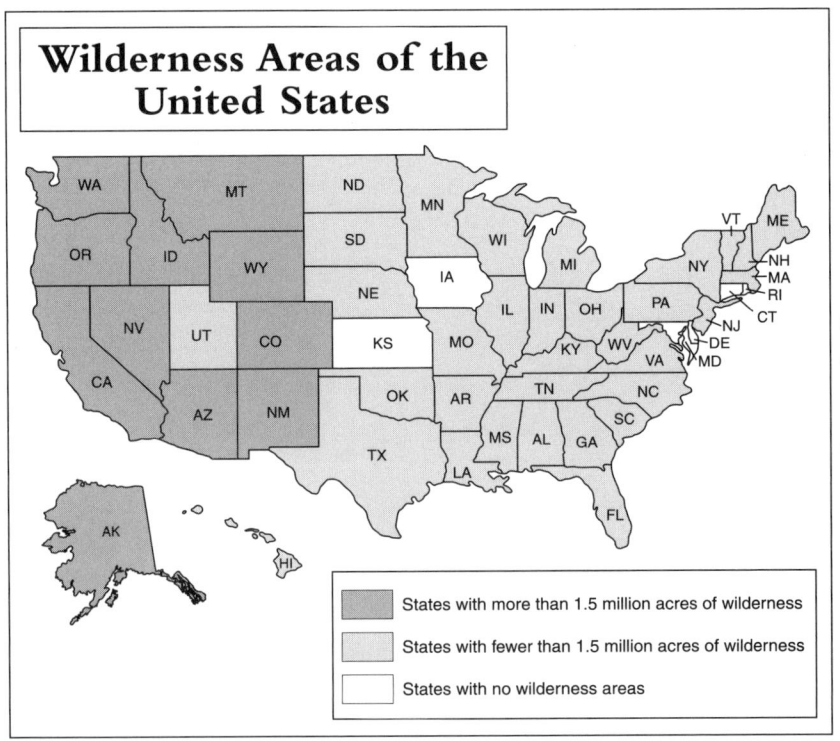

the strongest indicators of this change was the Wilderness Act of 1964, which set aside 9 million acres of land to be preserved forever untrammeled by humankind. Rather than attempting to perfect nature with human management, those supporting the Wilderness Act saw nature as perfect without man. By 2000 the amount of wilderness had grown to 105 million acres.

During this time, Congress passed a tidal wave of new legislation addressing environmental concerns and establishing new policies for the Forest Service and other public land management agencies. Americans wanted far more than just timber and water from their forests, and in 1960 the Multiple-Use Sustained-Yield Act sanctioned these demands. The Forest Service was required to provide outdoor recreation, rangeland, wilderness, wildlife, fish, timber, watersheds, and water flows. The National Environmental Policy Act of 1969 required that agencies such as the Forest Service apply environmental criteria to their activities. The Clean Air Act of 1970 and Clean Water Act of 1972 set new controls and standards for purity. In 1973 the Endangered Species Act guaranteed special protection to species at risk of extinction. The Resources Planning Act of 1974 required the Forest Service to assess the nation's natural resources every ten years and to set long-term goals. And finally, the National Forest Management Act of 1976 required each national forest to have a comprehensive planning process, to guarantee diversity of plant and animal species, and to allow for greater public participation.

New legislation required the Forest Service to consult with the public about management plans.

As this legislation changed how land, air, and water would be managed, a growing environmental movement determined to save nature from humans was making its presence felt. New legislation required the Forest Service to consult with the public about management plans. Organized environmental groups showed up in force at public meetings to air their views and seek changes in Forest Service plans that they believed favored timber production over concerns for forest health and biodiversity. By the mid-1980s the public input process was having a huge impact on forest management. Environmental organizations, timber firms, and the Forest Service engaged in long-running battles over timber sales, logging roads, stream protection, wildlife habitat, water quality, and recreational use. Kate Klein, a district ranger in the Apache-Sitgreaves National Forest in eastern Arizona, has seen her share of court cases: "Every time we lose a battle, we have to go back and do some more analysis, computer models and evaluations. It's a downward spiral. We're forced to do so much writing that we spend less time in the woods knowing what we're making decisions about."[19] Rather than spending time and money on the land, it was spent in courtrooms and on legal fees.

Do the Laws Work?

The new laws and regulations were intended to provide greater protection for the forests. Despite good intentions, in some cases these laws backfired and contributed to worsening forest health. The Blue Mountains in Oregon are an example of what went wrong. Holly Fretwell, a policy analyst who has provided congressional testimony on public land issues, writes, "Early travelers named the Blue Mountains for the constant haze of wildfire smoke that surrounded them. Frequent, small fires cleared the understory [of the forest], allowing the stately fire-resistant ponderosa pines to flourish. Wagon trains traveling west along the Oregon Trail rolled easily between the widely spaced trees of the forest landscape."[20] In a landscape that had once been defined by the constancy of fire, the Forest Service worked to eliminate fires.

Without fire, shade-tolerant firs grew up in dense thickets under the big pines. During the 1940s timber companies harvested the mature pines, which generate the most revenue, and left behind the crowded and weakened firs. This created the ideal habitat for the western spruce budworm, and the infestation spread rapidly. Immediate harvest and treatment could have saved valuable timber and might have prevented an epidemic. Instead, Fretwell explains that it took years for the Forest Service to respond. A maze of federal regulations and a lengthy public comment process slowed active management to a standstill.

Today the Wallowa-Whitman and Umatilla National Forests in the Blue Mountains are covered with "gray ghosts," 6 million acres of dead and dying trees. The lovely big pines are mostly gone, replaced with sickly firs unsuited to the dry climate and vulnerable to insects. In her book *Forest Dreams, Forest Nightmares*, Nancy Langston, an ecologist at the University of Wisconsin, explains how the dream of improving the forests with scientific management has led to the nightmare that exists in the Blue Mountains. She writes, "In trying to make the land green and productive, they ended up making it sterile. . . . It was a tragedy in which decent people with the best intentions destroyed what they cared for most."[21]

Instead of protecting the northern spotted owl, the Endangered Species Act seems to have inadvertently hastened the destruction of the bird's habitat.

The Endangered Species Act was supposed to protect the northern spotted owl in the Shasta-Trinity National Forest of northern California. To save the old-growth habitat preferred by the owl, the usual logging and thinning were halted. Mortality from root disease and bark beetles increased. As trees weakened and fell, fewer standing trees were left for nesting, and the dense, closed forest canopy was opened. Furthermore, the forest became more vulnerable to catastrophic fire that had the potential to wipe out the entire old-growth habitat in the area. In testimony before Congress on forest ecosystem health, Thomas M. Bonnicksen, a professor of forest restoration and resource policy at Texas A&M University, stated:

> By simply drawing a line around those forests and assuming that they're going to stay that way, we're setting up a catastrophe for the long-term viability of the owl,

because inevitably those forests are going to burn....
When we lose these forests or when they deteriorate, we
also lose the habitat we need for many of the wildlife we
value and we also further endanger species.[22]

Rather than protect the species, the act appears to have hastened the decline of the owl's habitat.

The Clean Air Act also has had an impact on forest management. Any fire that is deliberately set by a federal land management agency—a prescribed burn—must meet air quality standards just as a factory or power plant must. Ironically, the prescribed burns are intended to reduce the risk of much worse air pollution that would result from a huge and uncontrollable wildfire. It goes without saying that wildfires meet no clean air standards. Despite good intentions on the part of land managers, citizens still register complaints about smoke from prescribed burns. Although little research has been done on the effects of forest fire smoke on people, preliminary results from the University of Montana in Missoula indicate that high levels of fine-grain particulates are present in the smoke but not the cancer-causing compounds that are produced by slow-burning woodstoves. Even if serious disease is not a threat, burning eyes, runny noses, and sore throats elicit complaints that can go as far as Washington, D.C. When that happens, prescribed fires are quickly extinquished.

Private Versus National Forests

As we look closely at how the Forest Service, under the Department of Agriculture, manages the national forests and how other federal agencies, such as the National Park Service, the Bureau of Land Management, and the Fish and Wildlife Service, all under the Department of the Interior, manage their forests, it is useful to draw a comparison with how private forests are managed. In Gifford Pinchot's time, the young professional foresters chose to ignore the advice of experienced woodsmen at their own peril. Today public forest managers might welcome the advice of some of the country's private forest owners.

When Theodore Roosevelt established the national forests, he clearly stated that timber to build a nation, not beauty and wildlife, was the main purpose of the forest. Eighty years later, private industrial forests supply most of the nation's timber. Timber harvests from the national forests fell nearly 80 percent during the late 1980s and 1990s. "These [national] forests cover 192 million acres, represent about 27 percent of the nation's forested area, but currently provide less than 5 percent of the nation's timber production, a percentage that is falling,"[23] notes forestry expert Roger A. Sedjo at Resources for the Future.

Private industrial forests suffer few of the problems seen in the national forests. Boise Cascade owns a forest in the Blue Mountains that is managed for its timber values. It is free from dense undergrowth, sickly trees, and bug infestations, and it looks remarkably similar to the open forests of more than one hundred years ago.

Private industrial forests suffer few of the problems seen in the national forests.

Private forests adjacent to California's Shasta-Trinity National Forest are free from beetles and root rot and even provide habitat for northern spotted owls. In the South, the International Paper Company welcomes the public onto its timberlands. The fees that it collects from hunters, hikers, anglers, and campers have added significantly to the company's profits. With these incentives, the company is actively managing its forests for valuable timber as well as wildlife habitat and scenic landscapes.

Can these private forests provide valuable lessons for public forests? Should all public forests be managed for the same goals? Or should each be managed for its highest-valued use, such as timber, wildlife, or recreation, but not all of these values? Fires, too, have a role to play in each forest, but it is different for each one. Managing forests spread over such a vast and varied landscape with the same objectives and goals may not be good forest management.

A New Century

As the twenty-first century makes its debut, the extended drought in the West combined with warmer temperatures and overly dense

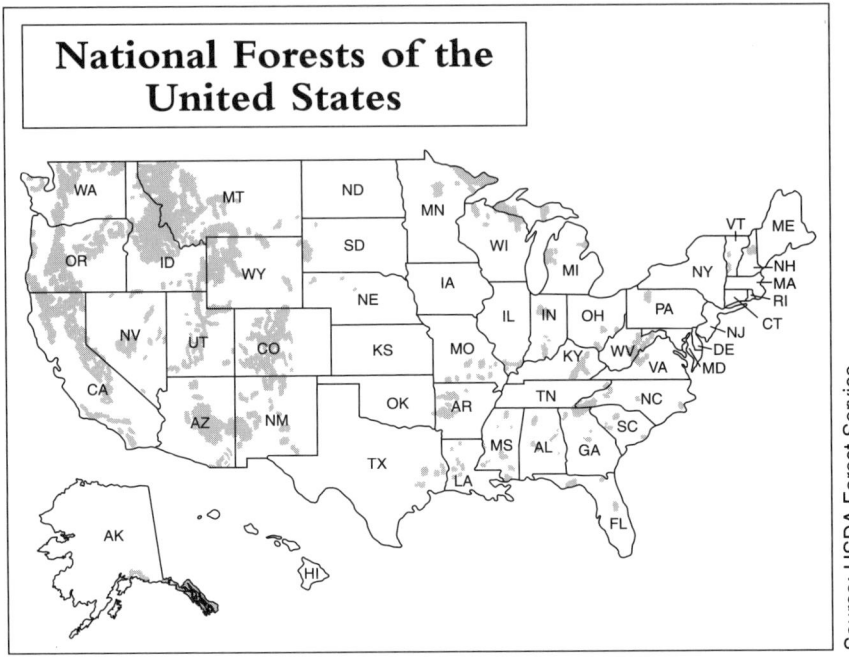

forests make uncontrollable wildfires a growing problem. The fires of 2000, the largest in decades, burned 8.4 million acres and prompted President Bill Clinton to establish the National Fire Plan. The plan doubled the firefighting budget and provided funds to treat 2 million acres at high risk to fire every year.

When Dale Bosworth took over as chief of the Forest Service in 2001, he announced that his agency was facing "analysis paralysis." By that he meant environmental laws and regulations were so numerous and burdensome that his agency was having difficulty meeting its obligations to carry out any on-the-ground forest management. According to a report from the government's General Accounting Office, the Forest Service was preparing more than twenty thousand environmental documents a year at a cost of $250 million. The public input process also was eating away at valuable employee time while the agency was attempting to deal with the increasing threat of wildfire. To address these concerns, President Bush proposed the Healthy Forests Initiative, which would have exempted small harvests and thinning projects from the public input process. Proponents of the new rules argued that more thinning would reduce fire risk while providing hundreds of jobs and saving valuable timber. Others were angry that the public would no longer be able to comment on and recommend changes to these proposed timber sales in the national forests. They viewed the legislation as a logging bill disguised as a forest health initiative. Perhaps it was both. The bill remained stalled in Congress at the end of 2003 and as yet there is no sign of a truce in the ongoing battle over public forest management.

Conclusion

Forest health remains a top concern for the future of public forests. Achieving this goal to a large extent relies on how the Forest Service manages fire. Having once declared war on fire, the agency is struggling to reverse directions and allow fire back into the forests while also fulfilling other obligations to provide recreation, water resources, timber, wildlife, and more. Whatever course is followed, most people would agree that past management practices have failed to protect forests for future use and made them more at risk to fire.

CHAPTER 3

Should Fires Be Fought?

The National Interagency Fire Center in Boise, Idaho, is the nerve center of the world's largest firefighting force. Every year from May to October, top-level fire managers monitor and direct firefighting efforts nationwide from the Boise headquarters.

The Forest Service, Bureau of Land Management, National Park Service, and three other federal agencies have joined efforts at the fire center, which occupies a fifty-five-acre campus with twenty-three buildings. The main warehouse can hold enough equipment to outfit twenty thousand firefighters and supply ten smaller regional warehouses. The shelves are stacked with flame-resistant shirts and pants, sleeping bags, gloves, boots, hard hats, goggles, tents, fire shelters, and so on. More than eight thousand handheld radios must be checked, which, during the busiest days of the fire season, can use as many as 385,000 batteries in a single day. Also on hand are thousands of generators, hand tools, thirteen hundred chain saws, and of course fire hoses—135 miles of hoses. The staff repairs, reconditions, and cleans all the equipment and then reissues it.

New Technology

The fire center's motorized forces consist of thousands of fire engines, bulldozers, and graders backed up by hundreds of helicopters, air tankers, and planes. New technology continues to enhance firefighting capabilities. One of the latest additions is thermal scan equipment for forest monitoring. Planes flying at fourteen thousand feet can detect a hot spot on the ground no larger than an eight-inch square and transmit that information to a computer on the ground.

Satellite signals provide a continuous flow of information to the center from more than eleven hundred robot weather stations placed in the forest. Meteorologists use the data to predict where fires will break out or how fires already burning might change in size or direction. When a fire starts, orders are sent to regional bases to mount an attack. Six mobile units, each packed with enough supplies for 250 firefighters, are ready to travel to the most remote sites at a moment's notice.

The government continues to increase the size and effectiveness of its firefighting forces and develop even more sophisticated technology. Annual firefighting costs are about $3 billion for the Forest Service and other federal land management agencies. From the public's perspective, these expenditures save lives, property, and natural resources that otherwise would be lost to fire.

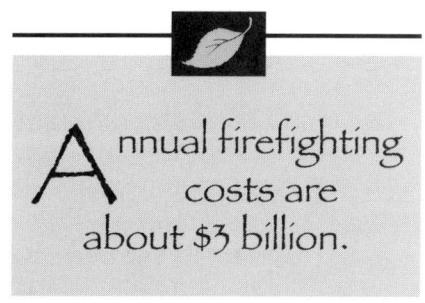

Annual firefighting costs are about $3 billion.

Success and Failure

The facts reveal many small successes and a few huge failures. Tens of thousands of fires are started on federal lands every year. Some are caused by humans, accidentally and intentionally, and others are ignited by dry lightning storms. Most of these fires are quite small, with 58 percent burning less than one-quarter acre, 88 percent fewer than ten acres, and 96 percent of all fires less than one hundred acres. A quick response, combined with moderate weather conditions, ensures that these fires are rapidly extinguished. Fighting small fires seems to be a solid success story.

At the other end of the spectrum, monster fires that spread over hundreds of thousands of acres cannot be stopped by even the world's best firefighting force. These giant fires represent just

2 percent of all fires that burn in a year, but they account for 94 percent of all the acreage that is scorched. Jack Ward Thomas, former chief of the Forest Service, was clearly resigned to the fact that when a fire "reaches a large size, putting it out is a joke."[24]

Ninety-seven percent of the money spent to fight wildfires goes to these relatively few immense fires. If these fires are going to burn no matter how much effort and money is spent to stop them, some suggest that a new approach to these blazes is needed.

Forest scientists have recommended more intensive thinning and even logging in order to reduce the amount of fuel in the forest that feeds huge fires. Reducing the number of catastrophic fires would cut firefighting costs. Secondly, the timber that is cut could produce revenues to help pay for more thinning, other restoration work, or, if necessary, more firefighting.

Many environmental organizations oppose thinning for fear it represents a return to the logging practices of the past where the largest, most fire-resistant trees—and the most valuable for lumber —were cut and the smallest, most fire-prone trees were left in

Dry lightning storms cause many fires every year. Most are small, but some consume hundreds of thousands of acres.

the forest. However, environmentalists often favor thinning around homes and communities if the harvest is limited to the smaller trees while preserving the larger ones. The Forest Service, the timber companies, and the environmental organizations continue to debate thinning with no resolution in sight.

Changing Public Expectations

If large, unstoppable fires continue to burn, why bother with firefighting? Fire historian Stephen J. Pyne contends that as American society has become more urbanized, it has become less familiar with fire and intolerant of its consequences. The public "came to view fire as social horror.... Its smoke they condemned as a health hazard. If they could banish it they would,"[25] Pyne writes. In a Forest Service document released in 1995, the agency acknowledged the need to include fire in forest management but also observed that the public had little understanding of the importance of fire to forest health. Early settlers were accustomed to the scent of wood smoke or even the red glow of flames on the horizon, yet modern day Americans perceive those same occurrences as far more dangerous and threatening. Simply put, the Forest Service is fighting fires because that is what the public expects it to do.

During the 1980s and 1990s, the West was the fastest growing region of the country. Entire communities popped up on the forest edge; the Federal Emergency Management Agency estimates that 38 percent of the homes built in the West are near forested areas, often called the wildland-urban interface. Until recently residents did little to fireproof their homes or businesses, and some have no insurance on their property. Others do not qualify for insurance because the roads leading to their homes cannot accommodate emergency vehicles such as fire trucks. The fact is that many people living in the forest and on the forest's edge rely on the federal government to protect their property and rescue them in times of crisis.

The "War on Fire"

For its part, the Forest Service considers firefighting part of its mission. The agency has been fighting fires since 1910, when the "war on fire" began in earnest. Thousands of people now make

Only a chimney remains of this house consumed by fire. As communities expand into fire-prone areas, more people depend on firefighters to protect their homes and property.

their living from firefighting and all the attendant services required by firefighters, from meals, showers, and refuse collection to helicopter and air tanker services. Entire rural communities in the West are dependent on the fire "industry" for their livelihoods just as communities in Michigan depend on the automotive industry. The federal bureaucracy that manages forest fires also has expanded and employs thousands of people. Consider the size of the Boise fire center and its ten regional facilities. Dismantling such an economy and the federal bureaucracy that keeps it humming would be an enormous task. It would devastate entire communities as well as businesses that specialize in firefighting services and equipment, not to mention thousands of families who would lose their source of income. Much like the dense thickets that fuel unstoppable forest fire, federal money is fuel for an economy built on firefighting; it, too, may be unstoppable.

Habitat Destruction

Although firefighting seems to have all the momentum, in recent years scientists, environmentalists, and even private landowners have expressed concern about the long-lasting damage to the landscape from firefighting. Efforts to stop fires can be more harmful than the fires themselves, according to Andy Stahl, director of the Forest Service Employees for Environmental Ethics (FSEEE). And the damage shows up in areas that the fire never reaches. A biologist watching a fire near Salmon, Idaho, lamented, "Between the Cats [bulldozers] and the retardant, they wiped out a lot of spawning habitat where the fires did almost no damage."[26]

Firefighting is perhaps the only activity conducted in the national forests that is not strictly regulated by environmental laws. Timothy Ingalsbee of the Western Fire Ecology Center says, "All environmental laws, standards and guidelines, regulations, and conservation strategies are suspended during fire-suppression incidents."[27] That statement may be a bit sweeping, but it indicates the wide latitude given to firefighters.

In the summer of 2002 the Biscuit Fire, Oregon's largest in more than a century, engulfed most of the Siskiyou National Forest and Kalmiopsis Wilderness Area, scorching nearly five hundred thousand acres. As the fire moved toward the home of Nancy and Gordon Lyford, bulldozers were sent to blaze a bare strip of earth called a fire line. By removing all the available fuel, the fire should starve and go out or at least slow down. The Lyfords' forty-acre meadow, which was near protected areas designated by the Forest Service and the Bu-

"All environmental laws... and conservation strategies are suspended during fire-suppression incidents."

reau of Land Management, contained an abundant variety of rare plants that had been tended by the local garden club for more than fifty years. The couple watched in stunned amazement as "just one bulldozer, then another bulldozer, then an ATV ... went smack through the middle of the meadow,"[28] says Nancy Lyford.

As it turned out, the fire never threatened the Lyford property, although others suffered devastating losses. The Lyfords remain grateful for the presence of the firefighters and accept the consequences: a scarred meadow and the loss of rare plants. Yet they cannot help but point out that an old road on their property might have been a better choice for the fire line. And if a biologist had been on hand, perhaps the bulldozers could have been directed away from the sensitive meadow.

Bulldozers topple large trees and rip out bushes and shrubs as they clear fire lines. In the aftermath, the bare earth is susceptible to erosion and sediment washes into nearby streams. The fire lines also make ideal habitat for non-native species that quickly outcompete native grasses and tend to be more fire-prone than the natives. These strips of cleared land that wander through the forest are an invitation to all-terrain vehicles (ATVs) that in effect turn the fire lines into unmaintained forest roads and contribute to erosion.

Fire camps composed of hundreds of firefighters and support personnel, dozens of vehicles, and tons of equipment leave a mark on the land. Often these temporary staging areas are larger than any rural town in the region. After visiting one such camp, an observer wrote that it "looked like a government-sponsored jamboree. People running around in red plastic vests, rented Ryder trucks, generators, computers, a kitchen being set up."[29] For added protection, the entire camp may be surrounded by a bulldozed fire line.

Skimming above the treetops, great lumbering air tankers dump hundreds of gallons of red fire retardant on the flames in a single swoop. Fire retardant has become an increasingly important part of the firefighting arsenal, but its safety is under scrutiny. According to government statistics, the retardant is 85 percent water and the rest is fertilizer and other harmless additives. Pilots are instructed not to drop the slurry near or in waterways, but in the heat of battle, accidents happen. Timothy Ingalsbee says the guidelines are meaningless. "The pilots are flying these World War II clunkers through billowing smoke and their number one objective is just trying to dodge a mountain, let alone trying to dodge a tiny stream, or the lakes and rivers below,"[30] he says. Further-

Firefighters bulldoze a large strip of earth to create a fire line around Oregon's Biscuit Fire in August 2002.

more, runoff can eventually wash the retardant into streams and lakes. The Forest Service typically uses 16 to 18 million gallons of retardant during the fire season.

Not everyone thinks the retardant is harmless. The Oregon Department of Fish and Wildlife reports that an accidental drop in Fall River killed more than twenty thousand native fish in a six-mile stretch. Studies have shown that benign substances such as coloring and rust inhibitors, when mixed together and exposed to water and sunlight, can create ferrous cyanide, which poses a threat to aquatic wildlife. The fertilizer in the retardant can run into streams, forming toxic plumes of nitrogen that kill fish and insects. The FSEEE wants the Forest Service to obey environmental laws even when it is fighting fires. The agency has failed to acquire permits for the retardants or the discharge of sediments into streams while bulldozing fire lines. The FSEEE intends to sue the agency under the Clean Water Act, the Endangered Species Act, and the National Environmental Policy Act unless the Forest Service complies with these laws.

Backfires are another firefighting technique more common today because they provide a greater margin of safety to the firefighters. Yet they also contribute to the total amount of acreage burned and pose a fire threat of their own. Backfires are fires intentionally set by firefighters to burn toward the oncoming fire, removing the fuel in its path and stopping the wildfire. Because the firefighters often set backfires several miles from the wildfire, they are at far less risk than when they are working on the front lines close to the blaze.

The downside to backfires is the additional acreage burned. In 1992 more than 35 percent of the land burned during the Warner Creek Fire in Oregon's Willamette National Forest was part of a backfire. Backfires can present their own danger because they are set under precarious conditions. A shift in wind direction can mean a whole new fire, not a backfire. According to residents of Montana's Bitterroot Valley, a backfire set in the summer of 2000 raced away from the original fire and destroyed ten homes that would have been unscathed by the wildfire.

Many facts suggest that firefighting efforts damage the land while having little or no impact on the worst fires. The Government Accounting Office, the government's investigative branch, reported that "large and intense wildfires are generally impossible for firefighters to stop and are only extinguished by rainfall when there is no more material to burn."[31] Eventually Mother Nature comes to the rescue with cool temperatures, wet weather, and calm winds. Certainly that was the case with the 1988 fires in Yellowstone National Park.

> Many facts suggest that firefighting efforts damage the land while having little or no impact on the worst fires.

Unlimited Funds

Some critics of federal fire policies refer to these monumental firefighting efforts against unstoppable fires as "political shows," suggesting they satisfy the politicians who appropriate the money and must answer to their constituents, but fail to put out fires. Economist, former Forest Service employee, and frequent Forest Service critic Randal O'Toole estimates that the budget for firefighting has increased more than 250 percent between 1980 and 2002. Andy

Charred household items and a scorched forest were all that remained after Montana's Bitterroot Fire, and a backfire set to stop it, burned out of control.

Smith, the chief of budget and evaluation at the National Interagency Fire Center, comments, "Although budgeted money runs out, it doesn't mean we stop fighting fires. We never stop."[32]

When money budgeted for firefighting runs out, as it frequently does, this does not mean that firefighters go unfed or unequipped or that bills to contractors for aircraft or support services go unpaid. Each year a certain amount of money is appropriated by Congress for firefighting. Once that money is used up, the Forest Service, for example, borrows from other categories, such as recreation, restoration, or research, to cover costs. During the summer of 2002 Patti Rodgers, a spokesperson for the Willamette National

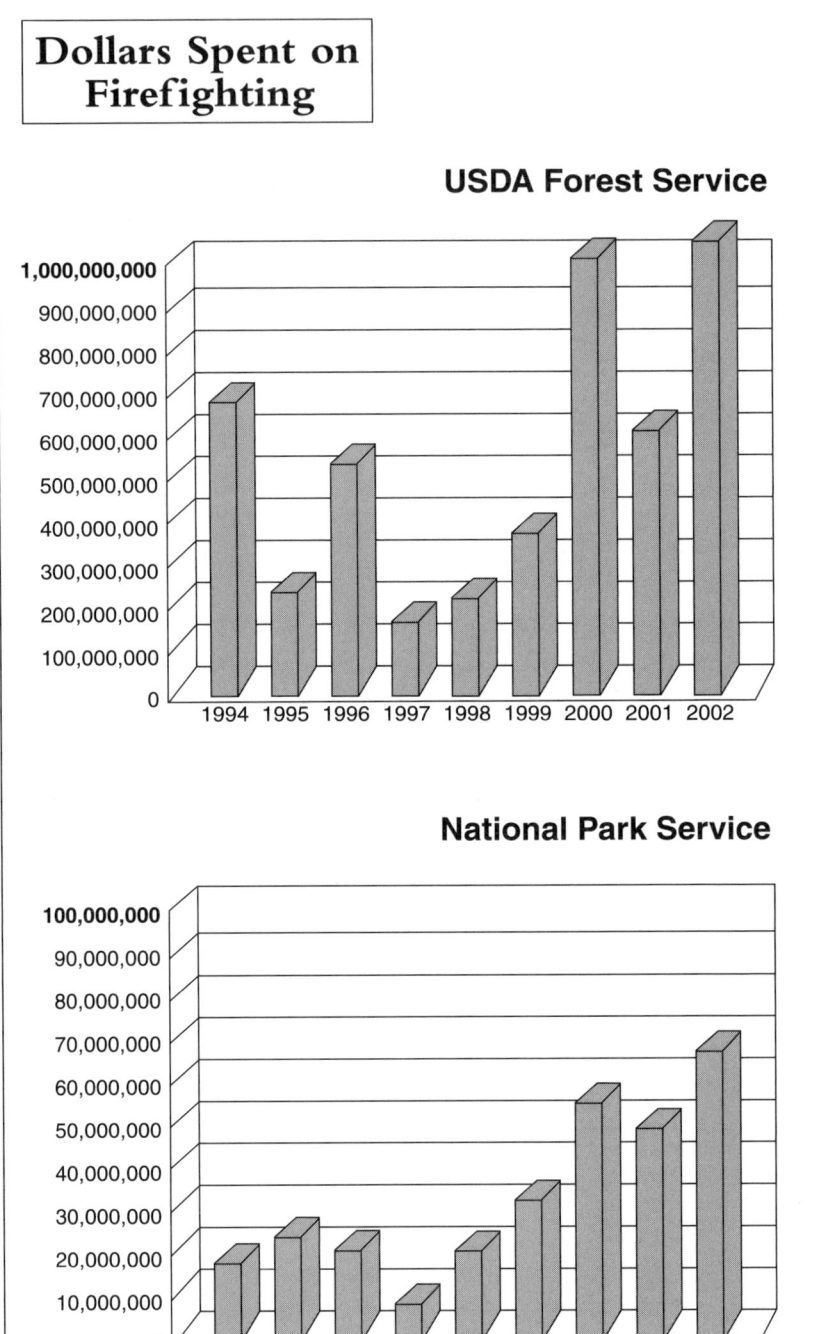

Forest, commented, "We're not going to stop fighting fire. What we're stopping is any noncritical spending. It means I can't go out and purchase a box of pens. Literally."[33]

Although the Forest Service may be out of money for a number of months and other programs can suffer, eventually Congress reaches into its deep pockets and reimburses the agency for its firefighting costs. These emergency funds have been unlimited during the past decade as well as at other times. The first indication that the bottomless bank account may be coming to an end surfaced in 2003. The Forest Service borrowed $919 million from other projects in 2002 to foot firefighting bills. Normally Congress reimburses the agency with emergency funds several months after the end of the fire season. This time, however, the emergency funds did not arrive until the spring of 2003, and then only $636 million was returned to the agency.

With basically unlimited funds, the Forest Service has had no incentive to control costs. Unwinnable battles with fire are fought. Air tankers are placed on seasonal retainers for $200,000, with additional costs of thousands of dollars per hour when the planes are actually flying. Brand-new trucks are leased from local car dealers for the duration of a fire and are then returned to be sold, reaping one dealer a tidy $1 million.

It is possible that if the well of money begins to run dry, some fires will be fought less aggressively and some of the most expensive firefighting activities may be curtailed. If the agency is forced to adopt a more cost-efficient approach, other projects to reduce fire risk or improve forest health might receive more attention.

Conclusion

Firefighting meets many human needs. These range from protecting lives, property, and natural resources to providing good-paying jobs and revenue for related businesses. Yet many aspects of firefighting seem at odds with the latest scientific evidence about how to restore forest health, including reintroducing fire to forest ecosystems. Even more striking is the low success rate for fighting large fires and the extraordinary cost that taxpayers shoulder for these failed efforts. If Congress does tighten the purse strings on firefighting, a whole new era of forest management and fire policy may emerge in the decades ahead.

CHAPTER 4

The Bitterroot Fires: A Case Study

The Bitterroot Valley, located in western Montana, is bounded by the Bitterroot Range to the west and the Sapphire Mountains to the east. The steep rock walls of the Bitterroots rise dramatically from the canyon floor. Meriwether Lewis and William Clark led the Corps of Discovery across these rugged, snow-clad mountains in the fall of 1805 on their epic journey to the Pacific. Today thirty-six thousand people make their home in the Bitterroot Valley. Missoula, Montana's second largest city, sits at the head of the valley, and the road south is dotted with bedroom communities and rural homesites at the forest's edge. Private forested lands and a growing number of homes border the Bitterroot National Forest for about 540 miles.

During the summer of 2000 fires burned 8.4 million acres nationwide, making it the worst fire season in four decades. Montana was hard hit, especially the Bitterroot Valley, where fires burned 355,000 acres, including 307,000 in the national forest. The National Interagency Fire Center reported that one in three federal dollars spent on firefighting that year was spent in Montana.

A close look at this valley and its summer of fire provides a better understanding of the problems faced by firefighters, homeowners, taxpayers, and the land itself. These fires are no longer unique. Where fire has been kept out, it is reclaiming its historic place. And when it does return, it does so with a ferocity that endangers both the people and the landscape they have come to enjoy. Yet as tragic as is the loss of homes, scenic landscapes, and valuable resources, the aftermath of the fire has brought its own calamities to the valley. Lawsuits and court battles have become as commonplace as the floods and noxious weeds. On the third anniversary of the fire, environmentalists, timber companies, valley residents, and the Forest Service continued to battle over the best way to manage the Bitterroot National Forest.

A Raging Fire Season

In western Montana the summer of 2000 was unusually hot and dry. When July lightning storms ignited more than one hundred fires within a few days, the fire season roared into life nearly a month early. Meteorologist Peter Flesch warned, "It is going to be a hot and heavy summer as far as fires.... We are comparing it to the drought of 1988." Even that early in the season, meteorologists were scanning weather patterns in search of rain. "There's no relief in sight,"[34] Flesch reported.

Flames light up the horizon as fire rages in Montana's Bitterroot Valley during the summer of 2000.

In the Bitterroot Valley, fires quickly doubled in size as more blazes started in the Bitterroot National Forest. Five hundred firefighters and dozens of fire engines, bulldozers, water trucks, helicopters, and air tankers were assigned to battle the infernos.

A week later fire officials announced that fires were breaking out all over the West, from California and Oregon to Utah and Colorado. Resources were already stretched thin. Thirty-five requests from national forests in Idaho and Montana for fire management teams and helicopters went unfilled. By now thirteen hundred firefighters were working the Bitterroot fires.

By the first week of August the situation had worsened. In the national forest ninety-four fires were burning, and in the Bitterroot Valley as a whole fires continued to spread virtually unhampered by firefighting efforts. The U.S. Army sent soldiers from Fort Hood, Texas. Canada sent ten of its crack fire crews. Weather experts arrived from Salt Lake City lugging a satellite dish, laptop, and solar-powered mini–weather station called a remote environmental monitoring system. "Nothing is unimportant when fire bosses plot the day's attack on a complicated set of wildfires, but weather may well be the most important. Weather dictates attack or retreat, safety or danger. In short, weather rules,"[35] wrote journalist Michael Moore as he reported on the Bitterroot fires.

The meteorologists scanned radar maps and downloaded temperature and relative humidity readings, wind speed, and wind direction. All of the weather data were fed to a fire analyst from the Forest Service with three decades of fire experience. The analyst added this information to other data on topography and fuels in the area. Firefighters returning from the front lines scribbled handwritten notes about conditions on the lines and passed them to the analyst. Using all of these sources, he tried to predict how dozens of fires would behave at certain times throughout the day. It is not a job for the weak of heart. The safety of hundreds of firefighters could depend on those predictions.

Loss of Homes

The weather continued hot and dry, and the fires grew. Hundreds of residents fled the smoke and flames, and others were ordered to evacuate. Schools opened to house the residents, and the Red

Cross set up aid stations. In the midst of the chaos, Max Baucus, the Democratic senator from Montana, arrived with Michael Dombeck, chief of the Forest Service, to see the fires and to be seen by the valley's constituents. They discussed the need for more thinning, more prescribed burns, and, of course, more money to aid residents.

Longtime fire bosses said it was the worst fire activity they had ever seen, and fighting the fire was made worse by the explosive growth of homes between the mountains and the valley floor. In Darby, south of Missoula, fire commander Steve Frye warned residents that homes would probably be lost in the next few days. "Unfortunately, that's part of the game of living in the woods,"[36] he said.

People at risk of losing their homes were angry, sad, and frustrated. Some said the firefighters were not being aggressive enough. "We're trying to protect those homes we can protect safely. These aren't the kind of fires we are trying to run out in front of and stop,"[37] Frye told the crowd, noting that in the past firefighters had sacrificed their lives to save property; that would not happen on his watch.

From their home in Coyote Gulch, Sam and Kathryn Minor watched as lightning slashed through darkened skies followed by plumes of smoke rising from the thickly timbered ravines and canyons of the Bitterroot National Forest. Like a lot of other people who moved to the Bitterroot, the Minors thought they had "found their slice of heaven, only to be reminded by Mother Nature that there can be hell to pay for living in the forests."[38]

As fires closed in on their home from three sides, the Minors knew the time had come to evacuate. In two cars packed with pets and day-to-day essentials, the couple hurried down the rugged dirt road to the paved highway, uncertain if their piece of heaven would survive the holocaust that swirled around them. Journalist David Foster of the Associated Press reported, "On both sides of the highway, flaming trees sizzle like slow-motion

> Longtime fire bosses said it was the worst fire activity they had ever seen.

A firefighter trudges uphill with a hose to battle the Bitterroot Fire. Thousands of firefighters spent six weeks trying to put out the blaze.

matches, in thirty seconds turning from green needles to black skeletons. Chunky embers whirl past their cars. The smoke is so thick they can barely see fifty yards ahead."[39]

Rain Brings Relief

By mid-August 265,000 acres had burned in the Bitterroot. The army sent more troops, five hundred from Fort Campbell, Kentucky, and another five hundred from Fort Bragg, North Carolina. By the end of August weary residents and exhausted firefighters scanned the sky for a few rain clouds, a cool breeze, any sign that a change in the weather would finally bring relief.

On September 2 Missoula's daily newspaper ran this headline: "Skies Pour Down Hope." Rain had finally arrived. Not just rain, but hail and wind and lower temperatures. The next day snow dusted the tops of the mountains, and fire crews made plans to pull out and head home. While some crews continued to work against the flames, others began to repair bulldozed fire lines. Mother Nature had accomplished in just forty-eight hours what thousands of firefighters and millions of dollars had been trying to do for more than six weeks.

Unnecessary Destruction?

With the fires in retreat, other problems began to emerge. Residents in the area around Dickson Creek are suing the Forest Service for destroying their homes with a backfire. In an effort to protect the homes from two wildfires, firefighters set a backfire to consume fuels and starve the oncoming flames. In this case, winds of forty miles per hour kicked up and pushed the backfire in the opposite direction that it was intended to burn. Within minutes, fire had jumped onto the hillsides and burned uphill, exploding into the forested area above Dickson Creek where homes were nestled among the trees.

The intensity of the fire incinerated ten homes. The area had been logged on three previous occasions and most of the homes were tucked into the thickets of regrowth. A few homes in the vicinity escaped the fire's fury largely because of broad green lawns.

Greg and Mary Tilford had lived in the area for ten years. They, like most of their neighbors, were uninsured. Their house was at the end of a three-mile stretch of winding dirt road that was impassable to emergency vehicles. Although the Tilfords say they accept responsibility for the risks of living in the woods, they do not accept being burned out by what they believe was a fire set by firefighters. They and their neighbors are suing the government for $54 million.

Although the Tilfords' case involved special circumstances, others living in and near the forests have lost homes and property to wildfires. James Witt, the director of the Federal Emergency Management Agency that summer, says the problem of living in harm's way is a growing one. Dennis Mileti, director of the University of Colorado's Natural Hazards Research and Applications

Information Center, agreed with Witt's assessment. After an interview with Mileti, a reporter with the Lee Newspapers wrote, "Those who settle in the West's remote forested valleys may have come to feel too safe behind the military-like firefighting protection offered by the U.S. Forest Service, which has nearly a blank check from government coffers to douse fires and protect rural homes with sprinkler systems, foam, and water-toting helicopters."[40]

The Price of Living in Harm's Way

The fact is that firefighters cannot save everyone's home, as the Bitterroot fires demonstrated, and more people are questioning whether that should be the role of firefighters. Should the federal government be expected to bail out those who have chosen to live in dangerous fire-prone areas? Should those who have chosen safe neighborhoods foot the bill for the lifestyle choices of others?

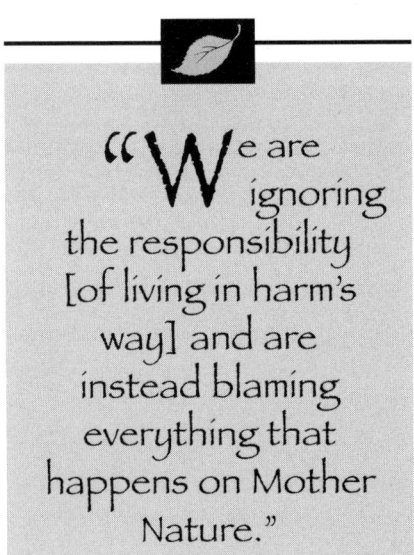

"We are ignoring the responsibility [of living in harm's way] and are instead blaming everything that happens on Mother Nature."

"There is nothing wrong with taking a risk if you are willing to pay for it yourself. This is a free country and I should be able to die any way I want. But the issue is we are ignoring the responsibility [of living in harm's way] and are instead blaming everything that happens on Mother Nature,"[41] Mileti says.

For homeowners who either have no insurance or not enough insurance, Mileti has little sympathy. He does not believe that the public should be held responsible for reimbursing those who have lost their homes at the forest's edge any more than those who lost their homes to a fire in a suburban subdivision. Taking this idea a step further, a public policy that would not require firefighters to defend private property would have profound effects on how fires are fought. It also would reduce costs and risks to firefighters.

Firefighters prepare to defend a cabin from an oncoming blaze. Many people question whether it should be the responsibility of firefighters to protect homes located in fire-prone areas.

Other Losses

Dealing with people who have lost their homes to fire is certainly an emotional issue, but equally devastating is the loss of a livelihood, which is often the case with farmers, ranchers, and timber lot owners. While fires threatening people's homes in the Bitterroot Valley kept firefighters busy, another fire broke out to the east. Because only timber and pasture were at risk, the fire was assigned a low priority. When initial attacks did not quell the flames, firefighters set a backfire that wiped out the one thing some residents say is more important than homes—food for cattle. Tom Liane, who works for Montana's Department of Natural Resources, says there is a saying about fires in cattle country: "Don't worry about my house; it's insured. Save my grass."[42] While home protection monopolized firefighting resources, elsewhere pastures and timber lots burned, threatening the livelihoods of many families.

Another problem faced by owners of agricultural land is invasive weeds that spread rapidly after a fire. Roger Sheley, an extension rangeland specialist at Montana State University, says that the longest-lasting economic consequences from the fires of 2000 could be the noxious weeds that destroy rangeland and cropland forever. The summer drought and fires killed off productive native grasses that can keep the weeds in check. Once weeds such as leafy spurge take hold of the land, they are almost impossible to destroy. The weed can send its roots twenty-eight feet down into the soil. Dealing with the weeds requires quick action. After summer wildfires, most ranchers have six months to get a handle on the weed problem before spring rains and snowmelt lead to a growth spurt, Sheley says. In one burned area of the Bitterroot Valley, the weeds were sprouting just a week after rain had put out the fire. Leafy spurge was already ten inches high.

Although ranchers know they need to attack the weeds immediately, herbicides are expensive. Likewise, there is not enough native seed available for reseeding. Government programs to fight weeds and rehabilitate the land move slowly through the corridors of power, and by the time they are available to people on the land, it can be too late.

A natural disaster such as fire seems to trigger a host of other problems in its wake. The same Bitterroot Valley residents who

After a fire, invasive weeds like these spread rapidly over burned areas, destroying farm and grazing land.

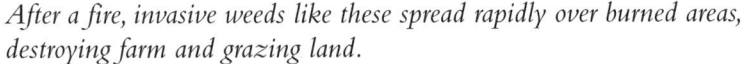

gathered in the summer of 2000 to hear the latest news about the fire returned in 2001 to hear the news about flooding.

Although the Forest Service sent in teams of forest rehabilitation experts immediately after the fire, the sheer size of the burned area—more than three hundred thousand acres, or half the size of Rhode Island—virtually guaranteed that treatment would be limited. Specialists examined the bare fire-scorched slopes and attempted to assess the areas of greatest danger.

Hot fires produce a water-resistant surface called hydrophobic soil. Although it is not permanent, it is particularly dangerous on bare fire-burned slopes. The soil cannot absorb rainwater. Instead, the water floods down the hillsides, carrying burned stumps, fallen logs, and other fire debris. The hillsides themselves are unstable without plant and tree roots to hold the soil in place. Large chunks of earth or even whole hillsides can break away and send mounds of mud and rock into homes and yards.

Restoration Plans

Even before the fires were out, both federal and state agencies were making plans to mitigate damage and restore healthy forest ecosystems. The federal government focused on the 1.5-million-acre Bitterroot National Forest and its more than three hundred thousand burned acres. Montana state agencies concentrated on the Sula State Forest, which is in the Bitterroot Valley and adjacent to the national forest. Even though the fires that burned the land were the same, the roads to recovery were vastly different. The federal government collected data, wrote a lengthy environmental impact statement, and held dozens of public meetings; the state foresters went to work on the land.

Wildfire burned twelve thousand of the Sula State Forest's fourteen thousand acres. Mark Lewing, who had worked on the Sula for twenty-six years, remembered the frustration of watching the forest burn as firefighting efforts were directed elsewhere. "The priority was structure protection and we didn't have any structures,"[43] he said. Yet after the fire, work proceeded quickly on the state forest leaving federal foresters feeling frustrated.

Like other state forestlands in Montana, the Sula must be managed for maximum revenues to support public schools. To fulfill this mission, the state was obligated to harvest the burned timber, replant, and return the forest to productivity as soon as possible. In order to get the best value for the fire-killed trees, they were removed quickly before rot and insect infestations further weakened them. By March 2001, 90 percent of the salvage logging was completed in the Sula, and $3.7 million in revenue had been deposited in the school trust fund.

Normally loggers would cut four hundred to six hundred acres of the Sula forest every year. After the fires, more than four thousand acres were cut, and towns in the valley were buzzing with activity. Stores, restaurants, and gas stations felt the flush of new money.

Meanwhile officials on the Bitterroot National Forest labored in their offices to get a restoration project under way. The Bitterroot Interagency Fire Recovery Team began its work in August 2000, held informal public meetings the next month, and by October was evaluating the forest conditions with the help of experts from across the country. A 350-page document was published in December with recommendations to reduce fuels in burned areas, improve watersheds, reforest, and sell burned timber.

Legal Skirmishes

As required by law, the public was invited to comment and ask questions. This process began informally in February 2001 and continued until the end of July with meetings, forums, surveys, and field trips to affected sites. A final environmental impact statement was released in October detailing the recovery plans. At this point the entire planning process started to fall apart as legal appeals and lawsuits began to fly.

Specifically, a coalition of groups including the Wilderness Society, American Wildlands, the Western Fire Ecology Center, the Center for Biological Diversity, the Sierra Club, and others objected to any commercial timber sales in the Bitterroot National Forest. More than a year of maneuvering passed before a federal judge ordered the warring parties locked inside the courthouse until they could negotiate a settlement. That settlement ultimately prevented the Forest Service from cutting any burned trees that were more than twenty-two inches in diameter. Afterward, chief of the Forest Service Dale Bosworth said, "I hope we have bottomed out. There has got to be a better way."[44]

Rescuers pull an environmentalist to safety after he lowered himself over a bridge to protest logging in the Bitterroot National Forest.

But even that settlement did not stop the skirmishes. Representatives from groups that opposed the timber sale carefully monitored salvage logging and restoration work in the forest. By June 2003 everyone was back in federal court to decide the fate of 199 trees. The Forest Service proposed to cut them because they were dead. The environmental groups objected. Living or dead, anything more than twenty-two inches in diameter was to be saved, according to the settlement. The judge sided with the environmentalists. When the fate of 199 trees on a 1.5-million-acre forest creates such animosity that it lands the opposing parties in court, it is a strong indication that the two sides also differ on many other aspects of forest management.

The ongoing battles in the Bitterroot are an example of what Bosworth called "analysis paralysis." The Forest Service estimates that the planning process for the restoration of the Bitterroot National Forest took the equivalent of three hundred full-time and thirty part-time employees for one year as well as the contracted services of hydrologists and other experts. It cost $1 million in public money and delayed active management on the burned forest for at least a year and a half. And after all that, it still ended up in the courts.

The public as well as the professionals are searching for more effective and more efficient forest management. As fires continue to blaze across the West every summer, the need becomes more urgent. "If we don't do anything, or we don't do enough, we're eventually going to burn up so much country that the problem will be solved that way," Bosworth says. "And that's a lousy way to solve a problem. It's not good for people, for wildlife, for soil, or for water when you burn these forests to bare ground. That's no solution at all."[45]

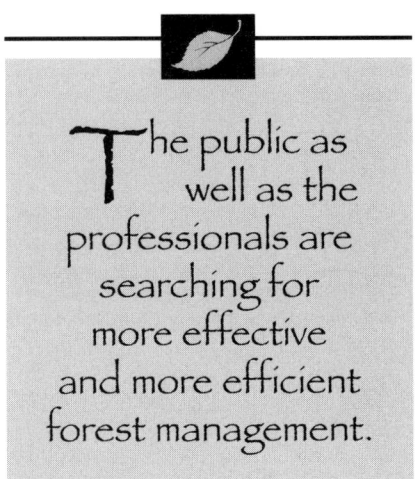
The public as well as the professionals are searching for more effective and more efficient forest management.

Conclusion

The story of the Bitterroot fires appears to be one disaster followed by another. Yet it provides valuable lessons to any homeowner who chooses to live close to fire-prone forests. Firefighters cannot protect lives and property from huge forest fires such as those that consumed so much of the Bitterroot Valley. However, new research shows that many homes in and near the forest can be protected from fire with proper landscaping and other simple techniques. Taking greater responsibility for private property not only will protect personal assets but also save the lives of firefighters whose job it is to fight forest fires.

CHAPTER 5

What Comes Next?

Americans have been at war with fire for nearly one hundred years. Efforts to eliminate fire from the forests have led to a crisis in forest health. Tens of millions of forest acres are in poor health, struggling with disease, insect infestations, and high tree density. The Forest Service itself estimates that some 70 million acres of land under its care are at grave risk of catastrophic wildfire and another 140 million acres are at moderate risk.

Ironically, eliminating fire has made forests more susceptible to fire—intense and uncontrollable fire. Fire historian Stephen J. Pyne says, "If you take the normal, historical rhythm of fire out, you get these kinds of horrific fires that scour out the landscape. These are of a scale and intensity and size that are just beyond the range of what the forest can adapt to."[46]

Scientists, land managers, and government officials all understand that to achieve healthy forests in the future, fire must play a role. The challenge is how to manage fire to benefit the forest and also provide human benefits such as recreation, water, and timber. Americans need to create a new model that works for the twenty-first century. Stephen F. Arno, a fire ecologist retired from the Forest Service's Fire Sciences Laboratory in Missoula, recalls the advice of George Hoxie, an early California timberman: "We had best adopt fire as our servant. Else it surely will be our master."[47]

Unquestionably, fire must be returned to the landscape, but there is no simple answer as to how this can be accomplished. Science can give us the facts about fire, but not the policies on how to manage it. The future of the public forests depends on how institutions such as the Forest Service put scientific knowledge to work.

The Ideal Forest

Part of the ongoing debate about returning fire to the forest focuses on what kinds of forests are ultimately wanted. What should they look like? Many people have the notion that the ideal forest is the one that existed before Europeans arrived on the continent. Others take this idea a step further and say they would prefer the kind of forests that had never been touched by man, completely wild and therefore natural.

Both of these visions fail to recognize two critical points. First, nature is dynamic, not static. That means woodlands are always changing. Glaciers, abundant moisture, violent storms, and fire all have an impact on the forests. Our forests today are responding

Smoke from a distant fire rises above a Montana forest. Scientists agree that fire is crucial to restoring forests, but they remain divided on how best to reintroduce fire to the landscape.

to a warming trend and drier climate. Different conditions create different types of forests. Over time, the changes have been so great that it has become impossible to re-create the forests of the past. Many of the essential raw materials may no longer exist, for example, certain seeds, soil types, microorganisms, and insects.

Second, these visions imply that forests were better, or more natural, without humans, who arrived in North America ten thousand years ago. Yet man is deeply intertwined with the evolution of the continent's forests. Pyne explains that many ecosystems in North America depend on fire, although some areas have little lightning activity. So where did the fires come from? The answer is humans.

Banff National Park in the Canadian Rockies illustrates Pyne's point. Berries, grasses, and other vegetation flourish in a landscape that depends on fire to create sunny openings in the forest, recycle nutrients, and germinate seeds. "The big, charismatic creatures—bears, bighorn sheep, elk—are all dependent on fire-created landscapes. But there's almost no lightning-caused fire in there. If we choose to stand aside and let nature do it [set fires], we're going to eliminate all these animals,"[48] Pyne says.

This does not mean that people should descend upon Banff and simply set fires, even though people are responsible for some of the West's worst fires in recent history. In the summer of 2002 a lost hiker set a fire to send a signal, and an unemployed firefighter set a fire in hopes of creating a job. Together those fires burned more than 400,000 acres of northern Arizona. That same summer, a Forest Service employee burned a letter in the forest on a dry and windy day, resulting in a fire that burned 139,000 acres of Colorado.

For many years people have differentiated between what they called natural fires and human-caused fires. The Forest Service, as well as other agencies, has had policies that allowed some natural fires to burn but called for all human-set fires to be extinguished. Yet over thousands of years the landscape has adapted to both natural and human-caused fires.

Reinstating Fire

Although the forests of the future may never resemble those of the past, the overriding goal is to ensure healthy, robust, and vibrant forests that can support a diversity of life. Because fire is critical to this goal, much of the debate about forests today revolves around how to reinstate fire. The possibilities vary widely, from the use of prescribed fire in small areas, to thinning and logging followed by fires, to letting the forests burn.

Pyne says simply allowing fires to burn will not work:

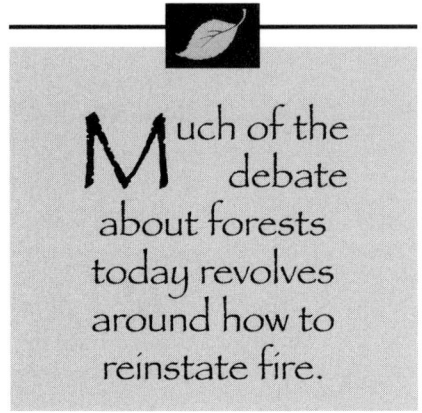

Much of the debate about forests today revolves around how to reinstate fire.

I think we've learned to our pain that it is not a reversible process. You can't put fire back in the same way you took it out. It turns out to be very complicated. It's like introducing a lost species: You can't take wolves and dump them into [a shopping mall] and expect that they are going to behave as they would have 200 years ago. You can't dump fire into some of these landscapes and expect that fire is going to dissolve all the ills out there.[49]

In the best of all worlds, each forest and each section of every forest would be restored according to its individual characteristics, including altitude, topography, climate, soil type, and so forth. Ponderosa pines would have cool-burning ground fires and lodgepole pines would have hot stand-replacing fires, but all this is not within the realm of possibility. "We're talking about boutique burning. Site specific, knowledge intensive, time intensive, and hugely expensive,"[50] says Pyne.

Logging trees and thinning the forest of dense thickets of smaller trees and woody undergrowth could be a first step to reintroducing fire. Without the huge amounts of fuel that now exist, fires would burn more within their historic ranges. This possibility has met with strong resistance from some members of the environmental community. Legal battles over timber sales in the national forests have tied up Forest Service plans for years in some cases. Many scientists and forest experts still see this as the best and most practical approach. New techniques for harvesting

Many scientists believe that logging trees is a necessary first step to reintroducing fire to the forests.

using smaller, lighter equipment would do less damage. Yet fears about past harvesting practices that damaged the woodlands have hindered efforts to pursue this option.

The "let it burn" approach is probably not the best ecological solution either. The intense fires burning today are unlike many of the past and can be more destructive than restorative. In addition, the destruction to property, the threat to lives, and the abundance of smoke would be unacceptable to most people. Smoke from summer forest fires was once a fact of life in the West, but now people recognize the health hazards of smoke as well as the damage it can do to the economies of many western towns dependent on tourism. It is interesting to note that in the summer of 2002 Colorado experienced a devastating fire season. After

Possible ways to reintroduce fire to America's forests range from setting fires in small areas to allowing raging blazes like this one to burn freely.

observing the fires from the air, Governor Bill Owens announced, "All of Colorado is burning."[51] The impact of this comment distressed some Colorado citizens as much as the fires. They blamed the governor for causing thousands of people to cancel their vacation plans to Colorado.

A Plan for Treating Developed Areas

A thoughtful approach to reintroducing fire has been proposed by Stephen F. Arno, who spent nearly thirty years as a researcher with the Forest Service, and lives on sixty acres of wooded land in Montana's Bitterroot Valley. Arno is well aware that protecting people and property in developed areas is essential before burning can take place. Because of the sheer magnitude of land that is in need of treatment, Arno proposes that government agencies concentrate on the 2 million acres that he says are near homes and communities. By treating these areas, he estimates that the overall costs of firefighting and damage to private property could be significantly reduced.

He suggests creating forested fuel breaks about one-quarter mile wide between forests and communities to reduce the probability of a severe wildfire. The fuel break would be cleared of most small trees as well as some of the larger trees with broad crowns (the uppermost branches) leaving a few tall trees of a fire-resistant species such as ponderosa pine. Ideally the crowns of the remaining trees would be at least ten feet apart to prevent fire from jumping from tree to tree and no more than 35 percent of the fuel break area would be under the tree crowns. This buffer zone would be far more open than most forested areas, but still not an eyesore. Fires approaching from the forest would be forced to drop to the ground upon hitting the fuel break because of the sparse and widely spaced trees. In some instances the lack of fuel might starve the fire. In others, it would slow the fire enough to give firefighters a chance to put it out or better protect the property in its path.

Arno has also given some thought to the costs of such a program, suggesting the larger trees could be sold as commercial timber and the smaller trees and cut branches could be chipped and bundled as biomass for use in industrial boilers or even in power plants to generate electricity.

In addition to Arno's suggestion of biomass, other new uses for small-diameter timber and undergrowth material that are so abundant in the forests are being developed by the Forest Service's Forest Products Laboratory in Madison, Wisconsin. Researchers have used wood fibers to make filters for streams polluted by runoff from farms and mines as well as combined them with recycled plastic to form a composite material for roofing, siding, doors, and even automotive parts. New technologies have made it possible to use small-diameter timber in construction where only large timbers had previously been used. Practical uses for this material would go a long way toward making large thinning projects economically feasible.

For the forested areas beyond the fuel breaks, Arno suggests prescribed fire preceded by thinning and the burning of slash and undergrowth to reduce the amount of fuel. He recommends mechanical treatments to move the forest toward a healthier composition and pattern. Mimicking the vegetative patterns that existed before fire suppression, a mosaic of dense growth and small openings or meadows could be created. And where appropriate, depending on the tree species, he would cut trees in order to leave a variety of different-aged trees. Once this task is complete, prescribed fire would be the next step.

Randal O'Toole, an economist and critic of the Forest Service, also sees development on the edge of the forests as one of the major problems facing fire management. Both he and Arno want to see more protection for human life and property before fire is allowed to burn or is reintroduced to the forest. It is accepted practice for the Forest Service and other government land management agencies to treat the land to reduce fire risk. O'Toole suggests that such treatments should not be the exclusive responsibility of the government. Private owners should assume more responsibility for protecting their homes and business properties. This would relieve the government of protecting private property, reduce firefighting expenditures, and lighten the tax burden for millions of Americans who do not choose to live in a fire-prone area.

Fireproofing Homes

Preventing homes from burning is Jack Cohen's specialty. Perhaps the world's expert on the subject, he is a research physical scientist at the Fire Sciences Laboratory in Missoula. After years of research, Cohen suggests a few simple rules for protecting homes from wildfire. First, use nonflammable roofing materials such as metal. One of the most common ways that a structure catches fire is from burning embers landing on a flammable roof. Wood shingles are frequently used in forest settings, but in Cohen's experience, they invite disaster. Second, provide a 130-foot cleared buffer zone between the sides of a structure and any flammable materials. The other most common way that homes catch fire is from flammable material igniting the outside walls. It is natural for people to surround their homes with native trees and shrubs, stack their woodpile against an outer wall, and allow fragrant pine needles to build up in the yard. Yet all of these are fire dangers. Forest trees and natural vegetation near the house are one of the worst fire dangers. A mowed lawn or watered garden would be a better choice.

A firefighter inspects a home for safety. Eliminating flammable materials, like the shrubbery around this house, is one way homeowners can protect their property from fire.

Cohen's recommendations are based on precise calculations. Even the hottest fire cannot ignite the outer walls of a home if it comes no closer than 130 feet. With that number in mind, he estimates that a 2,500-square-foot home with a garage would need a two-acre clearing free of fire-prone materials. Although the forest around the home might burn, ruining views and decreasing property values, it is highly unlikely the home itself would burn if these precautions were taken.

A new way of looking at fire protection could result from Cohen's research. Part of the Forest Service's preparation for firefighting is to map land with fuel buildup at high risk of fire. Cohen suggests that the agency is using the wrong criteria. Maps should instead reflect structures that are at high risk of ignition. If a home has been fireproofed as he recommends, it will not burn or need firefighters to protect it. To treat the land near developed areas is both inefficient and ineffective, says Cohen. It is inefficient because the critical area is much closer to the house and ineffective because fuel treatment will not stop flying embers from landing on a flammable roof.

"Instead of treating hundreds of millions of acres of federal land, we could treat only those lands immediately surrounding homes and other structures on the wildland-urban interface,"[52] O'Toole says. He estimates that 5 million homes would need to be treated, which translates into 10 million acres. Compared with the 70 million acres that the government says are at high risk of fire, O'Toole's plan would result in huge cost savings.

Responsibility of Homeowners

One problem with this solution is how to motivate private property owners, who now receive free fire protection from the Forest Service and other government agencies, to follow Cohen's recommendations. They might prefer to take their chances with the firefighters rather than pay to reroof their homes or to redo their landscaping. Yet as more homes go up in flames every year and TV news presents a steady diet of fire disasters, some homeowners are likely to make the modifications. O'Toole is even willing to go so far as to have the government pay half the costs because over time the cost savings in reduced firefighting would still be enormous.

Property insurance could help homeowners at risk and lighten the burden on taxpayers who provide assistance to those who are burned out. Although homes in remote forest locations do not always qualify for insurance, in more accessible areas insurance companies could require some fire prevention measures before a policy is issued. Nonflammable roofs and lots cleared of trees and shrubs would be Cohen's recommendations. At present, most insurance companies do not have rules for forest homes because the number of claims from wildfires remains tiny compared with the damages inflicted by hurricanes, earthquakes, and floods.

Another way to protect homes is through building codes enacted and enforced by local governments. Malibu, California, which suffered a series of disastrous fires, has enacted codes that dictate materials for roofs, walls, windows, and in some areas require indoor sprinkler systems. "Malibu homeowners face some of the strictest residential building codes in the country and fines for noncompliance,"[53] reported the *Washington Post*. The Los Angeles County Fire Department patrols neighborhoods to make sure homeowners have cleared away flammable brush. If residents do not comply, they face a fine of nearly five hundred dollars and a bill for a municipal brush clearing crew that can run as high as three thousand dollars.

California is not, however, the Rocky Mountain West, where many government regulations are still regarded with suspicion and disdain. Former secretary of the interior and former governor of Arizona Bruce Babbitt sees the benefits of more local controls:

> Living in the forest is dangerous, and ironically, in most of these areas there are no building codes at all. The governors and all the politicians are busy blaming everybody, but they seem unable to turn to the communities themselves and say, "You have a responsibility, and it's about time to enact some building codes and take some simple precautions." We still haven't learned that lesson.[54]

Family members watch a wildfire approach their home. Motivating property owners to take responsibility for protecting their homes remains a challenge.

A firefighter battles an oncoming blaze. Many experts contend that current firefighting policies are ineffective and perhaps even harmful.

Forest Service Reform

Even though the experts disagree on exactly how to restore fire to the forests and produce healthier forest ecosystems, most people can agree that current fire management policies are ineffective if not destructive. The Forest Service and other land management agencies responsible for fire management are so focused on firefighting that they seem deaf to the scientific evidence that forests need fires. When more than 99 percent of all fires are extinguished, despite a broad acknowledgment within their own agencies that more fires should be allowed to burn and that prescribed fire is an important tool for restoration, then surely something is broken and needs to be fixed.

Severe fires in the West automatically trigger politicians in Washington, D.C., to provide more money to agencies for firefighting. The Forest Service and other agencies keep on fighting fires and expanding their capabilities because the money keeps on flowing. Arno comments that "the old saw, 'If you have a hammer everything looks like a nail,' comes to mind in the face of a continued institutional culture within the agencies responsible for fire management. In spite of new recommendations for fuels management and prescribed burning, all-out suppression remains the blunt instrument of choice."[55]

Reforming the Forest Service is not a new idea, but it is certainly a recurring one as problems seem to be getting worse while costs are rising. Firefighting is a major source of income for the Forest Service. Without that task, the agency would shrivel, although reformers suggest that the Forest Service could be re-created to do forest restoration and to harvest timber in a more ecologically and economically sound manner. Others, such as Robert H. Nelson at the University of Maryland, have suggested abolishing the Forest Service and turning federal lands over to private entities such as the Nature Conservancy or other conservation groups in order to achieve better stewardship.

Most people can agree that current fire management policies are ineffective if not destructive.

Although Nelson's suggestion is probably too radical for the majority of Americans, O'Toole has another alternative. He proposes decentralizing the Forest Service and other land management agencies that operate out of Washington. The National Interagency Fire Center in Boise, Idaho, would have to go, too. Each federal unit of land from national forests to national monuments and national parks would become self-funding. Revenues could be generated from visitor fees, resource production, or other activities that were appropriate. The manager of each unit would decide what fires to fight and what fires to let burn while working within his or her budget without the unlimited emergency funds. Politics would be cut out because Congress could no longer appropriate more funds for firefighting every year, thus perpetuating the cycle of poor forest health accompanied by growing budgets.

Allowing more localized control might also result in better forest management and improved health. As Pyne suggests, the best type of prescribed burns would be site specific and knowledge intensive, which local management is more likely to provide than centralized management from afar.

Conclusion

Increased awareness of poor forest health as well as the spiraling costs of firefighting have focused the attention of many Americans on a problem that needs a solution. Science continues to expand our understanding of how forests work and what they need to thrive. It appears that government spending on firefighting may be hitting a wall and that private citizens at the forest's edge may be asked to assume more responsibility for their personal property. Government, by its nature, is unlikely to make any radical changes, but as ideas bubble to the surface from both experts and concerned citizens, reforms that ultimately benefit public forests may be forthcoming.

# Notes

Chapter 1: Forest Fires: Something New?

1. Rocky Barker, "Yellowstone Fires and Their Legacy," 1996. www.idahonews.com.
2. Quoted in Alan Carey and Sandy Carey, *Yellowstone's Red Summer*. Flagstaff, AZ: Northland, 1989, p. 11.
3. Quoted in Barker, "Yellowstone Fires and Their Legacy."
4. Quoted in Rocky Barker, "The Fires of 2000—Afterword," 2000. www.rockybarker.com.
5. Quoted in Stephen J. Pyne, *Fire in America: A Cultural History of Wildland and Rural Fire*. Princeton, NJ: Princeton University Press, 1982, p. 48.
6. Charles Kay, "Aboriginal Overkill and Native Burning: Implications for Modern Ecosystem Management," 1994. http://wings.buffalo.edu.
7. Kay, "Aboriginal Overkill and Native Burning."
8. Quoted in Stephen F. Arno and Steven Allison-Bunnell, *Flames in Our Forests: Disaster or Renewal?* Washington, DC: Island, 2002, p. 28.
9. Kenneth D. Frederick and Roger A. Sedjo, eds., *America's Renewable Resources: Historical Trends and Current Challenges*. Washington, DC: Resources for the Future, 1991, p. 87.
10. Frederick and Sedjo, *America's Renewable Resources*, p. 87.
11. SMOKEYBEAR.com, Smokey Bear campaign images. www.smokeybear.com.

Chapter 2: How Should Forests Be Managed?

12. USDA Forest Service, "Process Predicament: How Statutory, Regulatory, and Administrative Factors Affect Forest Management," June 2002. www.fs.fed.us.
13. Quoted in Jim Petersen, "A Clash of the Titans," *Evergreen Magazine*, Winter 1994/1995.
14. Quoted in Jim Petersen, "The 1910 Fire," *Evergreen Magazine*, Winter 1994/1995.

15. Quoted in Robert H. Nelson, *A Burning Issue: A Case for Abolishing the U.S. Forest Service*. Lanham, MD: Rowman & Littlefield, 2000, p. 31.
16. Quoted in Nelson, *A Burning Issue*, p. 4.
17. Nelson, *A Burning Issue*, p. 6.
18. Gifford Pinchot, "The Relation of Forests and Forest Fires," *National Geographic*, October 1899, p. 403.
19. Quoted in Paul Trachtman, "Fire Fight," *Smithsonian*, August 2003, p. 44.
20. Holly Fretwell, "Forests: Do We Get What We Pay For?" PERC Public Lands Reports. Bozeman, MT: PERC, July 1999, p. 10.
21. Nancy Langston, *Forest Dreams, Forest Nightmares*. Seattle: University of Washington Press, 1995, p. 6.
22. Thomas M. Bonnicksen, "Forest Ecosystem Health in the United States." Testimony to the House of Representatives, April 9, 1997. http://commdocs.house.gov.
23. Roger A. Sedjo, "The National Forests: For Whom and for What?" PERC Policy Series. Bozeman, MT: PERC, August 2001, p. 3.

Chapter 3: Should Fires Be Fought?

24. Quoted in Nelson, *A Burning Issue*, p. 36.
25. Stephen J. Pyne, *Vestal Fire: An Environmental History, Told Through Fire, of Europe and Europe's Encounter with the World*. Seattle: University of Washington Press, 1997, p. 58.
26. Quoted in Orna Izakson, "Burning Agenda," *Eugene Weekly*, August 12, 2002.
27. Quoted in Izakson, "Burning Agenda."
28. Quoted in Izakson, "Burning Agenda."
29. Quoted in Nelson, *A Burning Issue*, p. 36.
30. Quoted in Jeff Barnard, "Feds Could Face Lawsuit over Fire Retardant," Associated Press, May 7, 2003.
31. General Accounting Office, "Western National Forests," GAO/RCED-99-65. Washington, DC: GAO, 1999, p. 5.

32. Quoted in Todd Wilkinson, "Saving West from Fires Carries Big Tab," *Christian Science Monitor*, July 11, 2002.
33. Quoted in Izakson, "Burning Agenda."

Chapter 4: The Bitterroot Fires: A Case Study

34. Quoted in Betsy Cohen, "Firefighters Make Progress near Darby," *Missoulian*, July 17, 2000.
35. Michael Moore, "Tag Team Advises on Weather," *Missoulian*, August 1, 2000.
36. Quoted in Jane Rider, "Fires of 2000 'Unprecedented,'" *Missoulian*, August 7, 2000.
37. Quoted in Rider, "Fires of 2000 'Unprecedented.'"
38. David Foster, "Paradise Lost," *Missoulian*, August 13, 2000.
39. Foster, "Paradise Lost."
40. Rick Barrett, Peter Salter, and Ron Seely, "Living in Harm's Way," *Missoulian*, September 10, 2000.
41. Quoted in Barrett, Salter, and Seely, "Living in Harm's Way."
42. Quoted in John Stucke, "Ryan Gulch Efforts Get Thumbs Down at Town Meeting," *Missoulian*, August 18, 2000.
43. Quoted in Sherry Devlin, "A Time to Cut," *Missoulian*, January 21, 2001.
44. Quoted in Sherry Devlin, "Bosworth Hopes for 'Better Way' in Future," *Missoulian*, February 7, 2003.
45. Quoted in Devlin, "Bosworth Hopes for 'Better Way' in Future."

Chapter 5: What Comes Next?

46. Quoted in Wade Graham, "Burn It to Save It," *Los Angeles Times*, October 20, 2002.
47. Quoted in Arno and Allison-Bunnell, *Flames in Our Forest*, p. 182.
48. Quoted in Graham, "Burn It to Save It."
49. Quoted in Graham, "Burn It to Save It."
50. Quoted in Graham, "Burn It to Save It."

51. Quoted in Becca Blond, "New Sparks of Life Rise amid Ashes," *Denver Post*, July 1, 2003.
52. Randal O'Toole, "Reforming the Fire Service," Thoreau Institute, July 2002. www.ti.org.
53. Jeff Adler, "Western States Weigh Wildfire Safeguards; Rigid Building Codes Have Spared Homes," *Washington Post*, August 13, 2002.
54. Quoted in Graham, "Burn It to Save It."
55. Arno and Allison-Bunnell, *Flames in Our Forest*, p. 171.

Glossary

backfire: A fire set to consume the fuel in the path of a wildfire.

blowup: A sudden increase in fire intensity or rate of spread strong enough to prevent direct control.

brush: Vegetation dominated by shrubby, woody plants, or low-growing trees.

buffer zone: An area of reduced vegetation that separates wildlands from vulnerable residential or business developments.

control line: All built or natural fire barriers and treated fire edges used to control a fire.

crown fire (crowning): A fire that moves through the crowns of trees or shrubs.

drip torch: A handheld device for igniting fires by dripping flaming liquid.

dry lightning storm: A thunderstorm in which virtually no precipitation reaches the ground.

fire line: An area that is scraped or dug down to the mineral soil to remove fuel and act as a barrier to the fire.

fire season: That time of year when wildland fires are likely to occur and spread, threatening resources and requiring the response of a firefighting agency.

fuel: Combustible material, including vegetation such as grass, leaves, ground litter, plants, shrubs, and trees, that feeds a fire.

fuel moisture: The quantity of moisture in fuel measured as a percentage of the fuel's weight when thoroughly dried at 212 degrees Fahrenheit.

fuel reduction: The removal or burning of fuels to reduce the chances of fire or, if a fire occurs, lessens damages and increases the opportunity for control.

hand line: A fire line built with hand tools.

hotshot crew: A highly trained fire crew used mainly to build a fire line by hand.

infrared detection: The use of heat-sensing equipment to detect fires.

ladder fuels: Fuels that allow a surface fire to climb into the crowns of trees.

litter: The top layer of the forest floor, composed of loose debris, dead sticks, branches, twigs, and recently fallen leaves or needles.

mineral soil: Soil layers below the organic material with little combustible material.

prescribed fire: A fire deliberately ignited by managers under predetermined conditions to meet certain objectives, such as fuel reduction or habitat improvement. The fire must have an approved plan and meet environmental standards.

prevention: Activities directed at reducing the incidence of fires, including public education, law enforcement, personal contact, and reduction of fuel hazards.

rehabilitation: The activities necessary to repair damage or disturbance caused by wildland fire or the fire suppression activity.

retardant: A substance or chemical agent that reduces the flammability of combustibles.

slash: Debris left after logging, pruning, thinning, or brush cutting, including logs, chips, bark, branches, stumps, and broken understory trees or brush.

smoke jumper: A firefighter who parachutes to the scene of a fire.

suppression: All the work of extinguishing or containing a fire, beginning with its discovery.

uncontrolled fire: Any fire that threatens to destroy life, property, or natural resources.

wildland fire: Any nonstructure fire, other than prescribed fire, that occurs in the wildland.

wildland-urban interface: The area where structures and other human development meet or intermingle with undeveloped wildland.

This glossary was modified from an extensive fire glossary at the National Interagency Fire Center website at www.nifc.gov/fireinfo.

For Further Reading

Books

Stephen F. Arno and Steven Allison-Bunnell, *Flames in Our Forests: Disaster or Renewal?* Washington, DC: Island, 2002. A forest researcher tells the history of fire in the western forests, how it has been excluded, and how we can bring it back.

Jim Carrier, *Summer of Fire*. Salt Lake City: Gibbs Smith, 1989. A chronicle of the 1988 Yellowstone fires.

Stephen J. Pyne, *Fire in America: A Cultural History of Wildland and Rural Fire*. Princeton, NJ: Princeton University Press, 1982. Examines the ways in which humans have used fire through history.

Periodical

Charles Mann, "1491," *Atlantic Monthly*, March 2002.

Websites

Forest Service Fire Sciences Lab, http://firelab.org.

National Interagency Fire Center, www.nifc.gov.

PBS, "Fire Wars," *NOVA*, www.pbs.org/wgbh/nova/fire.

SMOKEYBEAR.com, www.smokeybear.com.

Western Fire Ecology Center, www.fire-ecology.org.

Works Consulted

Books

Robert Barbee, *The Great Yellowstone Fires of 1988*. Salt Lake City: Gibbs Smith, 1989.

Thomas M. Bonnicksen, *America's Ancient Forests: From the Ice Age to the Age of Discovery*. New York: John Wiley & Sons, 2000.

Robert Boyd, ed., *Indians, Fire, and the Land in the Pacific Northwest*. Corvallis: Oregon State University Press, 1999.

Stephen Budiansky, *Nature's Keepers: The New Science of Nature Management*. New York: Free, 1995.

Alan Carey and Sandy Carey, *Yellowstone's Red Summer*. Flagstaff, AZ: Northland, 1989.

John Fedkiw, *Managing Multiple Uses on National Forests, 1905–1995: A Ninety-Year Learning Experience and It Isn't Finished Yet*. Washington, DC: USDA Forest Service, FS-628, 1998.

Kenneth D. Frederick and Roger A. Sedjo, eds., *America's Renewable Resources: Historical Trends and Current Challenges*. Washington, DC: Resources for the Future, 1991.

Nancy Langston, *Forest Dreams, Forest Nightmares*. Seattle: University of Washington Press, 1995.

Donald R. Leal and Roger E. Meiners, eds., *Government vs. Environment*. Lanham, MD: Rowman & Littlefield, 2002.

Micah Morrison, *Fire in Paradise: The Yellowstone Fires and the Politics of Environmentalism*. New York: HarperCollins, 1993.

Robert H. Nelson, *A Burning Issue: A Case for Abolishing the U.S. Forest Service*. Lanham, MD: Rowman & Littlefield, 2000.

Randal O'Toole, *Reforming the Forest Service*. Washington, DC: Island, 1988.

Stephen J. Pyne, *Fire: A Brief History*. Seattle: University of Washington Press, 2001.

———, *Vestal Fire: An Environmental History, Told Through Fire, of Europe and Europe's Encounter with the World*. Seattle: University of Washington Press, 1997.

———, *Year of the Fires: The Story of the Great Fires of 1910*. New York: Viking, 2001.

George Wuerthner, *Yellowstone and the Fires of Change*. Salt Lake City: Haggis House, 1988.

Periodicals

Jeff Adler, "Western States Weigh Wildfire Safeguards; Rigid Building Codes Have Spared Homes," *Washington Post*, August 13, 2002.

Bob Anez, "State Officials Assail FS Burn Policy," *Missoulian*, October 4, 2001.

Jeff Barnard, "Feds Could Face Lawsuit over Fire Retardant," Associated Press, May 7, 2003.

Rick Barrett, Peter Salter, and Ron Seely, "Living in Harm's Way," *Missoulian*, September 10, 2000.

Becca Blond, "New Sparks of Life Rise Amid Ashes," *Denver Post*, July 1, 2003.

Rob Chaney, "Autumn in Ashes," *Missoulian*, October 1, 2000.

———, "Rain Slickens Terrain, Dampens Area Fires," *Missoulian*, September 3, 2000.

Betsy Cohen, "Firefighters Make Progress near Darby," *Missoulian*, July 17, 2000.

Jack D. Cohen, "Preventing Disaster, Home Ignitability in the Wildland-Urban Interface," *Journal of Forestry*, 1998.

Sherry Devlin, "Agency's Budget Ravaged," *Missoulian*, October 29, 2002.

———, "Appeal Filed on Salvage," *Missoulian*, February 1, 2002.

———, "Bitterroot Forest: Environmentalists Say Let Nature Heal Itself," *Missoulian*, May 25, 2001.

———, "Bitterroot Forest Supervisor Hears Praise, Complaints," *Missoulian*, August 13, 2000.

———, "Bitterroot National Forest Issues Final EIS," *Missoulian*, October 11, 2001.

———, "Bosworth Hopes for 'Better Way' in Future," *Missoulian*, February 7, 2003.

———, "Bringing Back the Bitterroot," *Missoulian*, February 7, 2001.

———, "Check with Reality," *Missoulian*, August 22, 2000.

———, "Clear Picture of Filthy Air," *Missoulian*, February 4, 2001.

———, "Duty Well Done," *Missoulian*, September 13, 2000.

———, "Endangered Forests List Draws Retort from Supervisor," *Missoulian*, June 6, 2003.

———, "Environmentalists Say They Will Accept Some Logging on the Bitterroot Forest," *Missoulian*, February 5, 2002.

———, "Fire Officials Fear the Worst Is on the Way," *Missoulian*, July 26, 2000.

———, "Fires of 2000: Martz Says Feds Should Start Salvage," *Missoulian*, March 9, 2001.

———, "Forest Service Turns Eye Toward Flood Threat," *Missoulian*, September 2, 2000.

———, "Judge Orders Mediation over Timber," *Missoulian*, February 2, 2002.

———, "Local Authors Address Forest Living, Fire," *Missoulian*, May 26, 2002.

———, "Menace in Waiting," *Missoulian*, August 21, 2000.

———, "Officials Delay Ruling on Bitterroot Logging," *Missoulian*, November 20, 2001.

———, "Public Packs Salvage Timber Hearing," *Missoulian*, January 4, 2002.

———, "Ruling Protects Dead Bitterroot Trees," *Missoulian*, June 27, 2003.

———, "A Time to Cut," *Missoulian*, January 21, 2001.

———, "Valley Bound to Burn, Say Officials," *Missoulian*, August 8, 2000.

Jan Falstad, "Fires May Leave Legacy of Weeds," *Missoulian*, October 22, 2000.

———, "Tracking the Bill," *Missoulian*, October 22, 2000.

David Foster, "Paradise Lost," *Missoulian*, August 13, 2000.

Daryl Gadbow, "Residents Sue over Bitterroot Fires," *Missoulian*, July 23, 2002.

Susan Gallagher, "More Troops Sent to Fight State's Fires," *Missoulian*, August 26, 2000.

Wade Graham, "Burn It to Save It," *Los Angeles Times*, October 20, 2002.

Orna Izakson, "Burning Agenda," *Eugene Weekly*, August 12, 2002.

Daniel Kemmis, "Working with Gridlock," *Missoulian*, December 30, 2001.

Jake Krelick, "We Must Learn from Past Mistakes in the Bitterroot National Forest," *Missoulian*, December 10, 2001.

Ginger Merriam, "Bitterroot Fire Biggest in Nation," *Missoulian*, August 29, 2000.

Michael Moore, "Tag Team Advises on Weather," *Missoulian*, August 1, 2000.

Michael Moore et al., "Skies Pour Down Hope," *Missoulian*, September 2, 2000.

Patrick Orr, "About NIFC," *Idaho Statesman*, June 8, 2003.

———, "The Business of NIFC," *Idaho Statesman*, June 8, 2003.

———, "NIFC History," *Idaho Statesman*, June 8, 2003.

———, "NIFC Partners," *Idaho Statesman*, June 8, 2003.

———, "When Wildfires Heat Up Who Ya Gonna Call? NIFC," *Idaho Statesman*, June 8, 2003.

Jim Petersen, "A Clash of the Titans," *Evergreen Magazine*, Winter 1994/1995.

———, "The 1910 Fire," *Evergreen Magazine*, Winter 1994/1995.

Gifford Pinchot, "The Relation of Forests and Forest Fires," *National Geographic*, October 1899.

Stephen J. Pyne, "The Big Blowup," *High Country News*, April 23, 2001.

Jane Rider, "Fires May Force New Building Regs," *Missoulian*, December 23, 2000.

———, "Fires of 2000: Models of Landscape," *Missoulian*, December 31, 2000.

———, "Fires of 2000 'Unprecedented,'" *Missoulian*, August 7, 2000.

———, "Frustrations Mount over Bitterroot Flooding," *Missoulian*, July 26, 2001.

———, "Large-Scale Restoration Project Under Way on Ranch near Darby," *Missoulian*, November 26, 2000.

———, "Losing More Ground," *Missoulian*, August 5, 2000.

Ray Ring, "A Losing Battle," *High Country News*, May 26, 2003.

Chris Risbrudt, "Four-Part Plan—Forest Service Focuses on Quartet of Threats to Habitat Health," *Missoulian*, June 19, 2003.

Scott Sonner, "Congress Unlikely to Fully Fund Forest Service," *Reno Gazette Journal*, May 7, 2003.

John Strommes, "Restoring State Land a Priority," *Missoulian*, September 9, 2000.

John Stucke, "Ryan Gulch Efforts Get Thumbs Down at Town Meeting," *Missoulian*, August 18, 2000.

Paul Trachtman, "Fire Fight," *Smithsonian*, August 2003.

Todd Wilkinson, "Saving West from Fires Carries Big Tab," *Christian Science Monitor*, July 11, 2002.

Internet Sources

American Park Network, "Sequoia and Kings Canyon Flora and Fauna." www.americanparknetwork.com.

Rocky Barker, "The Fires of 2000—Afterword," 2000. www.rockybarker.com.

———, "Yellowstone Fires and Their Legacy," 1996. www.idahonews.com.

Thomas M. Bonnicksen, "Forest Ecosystem Health in the United States." Testimony to the House of Representatives, April 9, 1997. http://commdocs.house.gov.

Jack D. Cohen, "Examination of the Home Destruction in Los Alamos Associated with the Cerro Grande Fire, July 10, 2000." www.firelab.org.

———, "What Is the Wildland Fire Threat to Homes?" Thompson Memorial Lecture, School of Forestry Northern Arizona University, April 10, 2000. www.firelab.org.

Sally M. Haase and Stephen S. Sackett, "Effects of Prescribed Fire in Giant Sequoia–Mixed Conifer Stands in Sequoia and Kings Canyon National Parks," 1998. www.nps.gov.

Holly Hartman, "Smokey Bear: A Friend of Our Forests for More than Half a Century." www.factmonster.com.

Timothy Ingalsbee, "Money to Burn: The Economics of Fire and Fuels Management, Part One: Suppression," Western Fire Ecology Center, 2000. www.fire-ecology.org.

Charles E. Kay, "Aboriginal Overkill and Native Burning: Implications for Modern Ecosystem Management," 1994. http://wings.buffalo.edu.

Bruce M. Kilgore, "Fire's Role in a Sequoia Forest." www.nps.gov.

National Interagency Fire Center, "National Fire Plan." www.nifc.gov.

Randal O'Toole, "Reforming the Fire Service," Thoreau Institute, July 2002. www.ti.org.

PBS, "Fire Wars," *NOVA*, May 9, 2002. www.pbs.org.

Jim Petersen, "The West Is Burning Up!" www.idahoforests.org.

Ryan Shaffer, "Conservation Groups and Bitterroot Residents Unite to Oppose Timber Sale." www.wildrockiesalliance.org.

SMOKEYBEAR.com, "Smokey's Vault." www.smokeybear.com.

USDA Forest Service, "Fire and Aviation Management." www.fs.fed.us.

———, "Grey Towers National Historic Landmark." www.fs.fed.us.

———, "Process Predicament: How Statutory, Regulatory, and Administrative Factors Affect Forest Management," June 2002. www.fs.fed.us.

USGS Biological Resources, "Effects of Fire Suppression on Ecosystems and Diversity." http://biology.usgs.gov.

USGS Western Ecological Research Center, "Fire and Sequoia Reproduction." www.werc.usgs.gov.

Wildfire News, "No More Retardant? Enviros Plan to Sue," May 8, 2003. www.wildfirenews.com.

Reports

General Accounting Office, "Western National Forests." GAO/RCED-99-65. Washington, DC: GAO, 1999.

Holly Fretwell, "Forests: Do We Get What We Pay For?" PERC Public Lands Report. Bozeman, MT: PERC, July 1999.

Roger A. Sedjo, "The National Forests: For Whom and for What?" PERC Policy Series. Bozeman, MT: PERC, 2001.

Acknowledgments

Critical Thinking About Environmental Issues: *Forest Fires*, by Linda E. Platts, is part of a series designed to objectively discuss environmental issues. The editor of the series, Jane S. Shaw, particularly appreciates the support of two people who recognize the value of treating issues in a fair, balanced, and thorough way. They are Fred L. Smith Jr., president of the Competitive Enterprise Institute in Washington, D.C., and Terry L. Anderson, executive director of PERC—the Center for Free Market Environmentalism—in Bozeman, Montana. She also thanks Michael Sanera, for his role in initiating this series, and the Grover Hermann Foundation and the Bass Foundation for their support. Linda E. Platts appreciates the advice of Shaw in completing this book and the help of PERC's Michelle McReynolds.

Index

agriculture, 17, 57–58
American Wildlands, 60
analysis paralysis, 62
animals
 dependent on fire-created habitats, 65
 effect of forest fires on, 12, 13
 Endangered Species Act and, 31, 33–34
 fire retardant and, 45
Arno, Stephen F., 63, 68–70, 75
ash, minerals in, 13

Babbitt, Bruce, 73
backfires, 45–46, 55
Bambi (movie), 19–20
Banff National Park (Canada), 65
Barker, Rocky, 10
Barkley, Carree, 13
Baucus, Max, 53
Big Blowup of 1910, 19, 26
Biscuit Fire (Oregon), 43–44
Bitterroot fires (Montana)
 acreage burned by, 50
 backfire destruction during, 46
 conditions leading to, 51
 ecological effects of, 57–59
 land rehabilitation and, 59–62
 wildland-urban interface communities and, 52–54, 55
Bitterroot Interagency Fire Recovery Team, 60
Bitterroot National Forest
 prescribed burns in, 22
 timber sales from, 60–62
 see also Bitterroot fires
Blue Mountains (Oregon), 32–33, 35

Boise, Idaho, 38, 42
Boise Cascade, 35
Bonnicksen, Thomas, 33–34
Bosworth, Dale, 36, 60, 62
Bunnell, David, 23
Bureau of Land Management, 9, 28, 38
Burning and Empire (Holbrook), 26

Center for Biological Diversity, 60
Clark, William, 16
Clark-McNary Act (1924), 19
Clean Air Act (1970), 31, 34
Clean Water Act (1972), 31
Clinton, Bill, 35–36
Cohen, Jack, 70–72

Department of Agriculture, 21, 34
Department of the Interior, 34
Despain, Don, 12
Dombeck, Michael, 53
drip torches, 22

Endangered Species Act (1973), 31, 33–34
environmental legislation
 effects of, 33–34
 land rehabilitation and, 59, 60–62
 logging and, 32–33, 36–37
 requirements of, 30–32
 suspension of, during firefighting, 43, 44
environmental organizations, 40–41, 60–62, 75
erosion, 44

Federal Emergency Management
  Agency, 41
firefighting
  case against, 28
  cost of
    annually, 26–27, 39
    availability of funds, 18, 49
    increase in, 46–47
    National Fire Plan and, 36
  fire size and success of, 39–40,
    46, 55, 63
  government agencies
    responsible for, 9, 28, 38
  habitat destruction during,
    43–46
  as income source for Forest
    Service, 75
  industry, 21, 42–43, 75
  policy basis of, 65
  as scientific management, 27
  suspension of environmental
    legislation during, 43, 44
  technology, 28, 38–40, 52
fire lines, 43, 44
fire retardant, 44–45
fires
  acreage at risk for, 63
  acreage burned
    annual, 40
    pattern of, 23
    in 2000, 35–36, 50
  as annual events, 62
  change in nature of, 23–24
  ecological effects of
    negative, 57–59
    positive, 9, 23, 29–30
  natural
    causes of, 13, 15
    colonists and, 16
    increase in uncontrollable,
      35–36
    pattern of, 15
  preventing, 19–21
  reinstating, 65–70
  started by humans
    backfires, 45–46, 55
    as management tool used by
      Indians, 13–16
    prescribed burns
      best type of, 76
      Clean Air Act and, 34
      purpose of, 23
      techniques used in, 22
      in wildland-urban interface
        communities, 69–70
      set in 2002, 65
      settlers and, 16–17
      Smokey Bear and, 21
Fire Sciences Laboratory, 70
Fish and Wildlife Service, 9
Flesch, Peter, 51
flooding, 59
Forest Dreams, Forest Nightmares
  (Langston), 33
Forest Reserve Act (1891), 18
forests
  development of, 16, 24
  economic value of, 25
  in Europe, 26
  ideal, 64–65
  national
    acreage of, 9
    timber harvesting from, 34–35
  old-growth, 16
  private industrial, 35
  see also wildland-urban
    interface communities; *specific
    national forests*
Forest Service
  acreage responsible for, 9
  after Big Blowup of 1910,
    26–27
  controlling costs by, 47, 49
  environmental movement and,

31–32, 36–37
firefighting as income source for, 75
fire prevention symbols of, 19–21
Forest Products Laboratory, 69
founding of, 18, 25
goals of, 18, 23, 25–27, 30, 41–42
lawsuits against, 45, 55
National Fire Center and, 38
reform of, 74–76
Forest Service Employees for Environmental Ethics (FSEEE), 43, 45
Foster, David, 53–54
Fretwell, Holly, 32
Frye, Steve, 53
fuel
  fire lines and, 43
  Indian management techniques and amount of, 15–16
  logging to control amount of, 40–41, 66–67
  relationship to nature of fire size, 24
fuel breaks, preventive, 69

Greeley, William, 27

habitat
  animals dependent on fire-created, 65
  destruction of
    by firefighters, 43–46
    lawsuits against Forest Service for, 45, 55
  natural rehabilitation of, 15
Holbrook, Stewart, 26
homes. *See* wildland-urban interface communities
Hoxie, George, 63

Ingalsbee, Timothy, 43, 44
International Paper Company, 35

Kalmiopsis Wilderness Area (Oregon), 43–44
Kay, Charles, 15, 16
Kings Canyon National Park (California), 30
Klein, Kate, 32

Laboratory of Tree-Ring Research (University of Arizona), 29
land, rehabilitation of, 58, 59–62
Langston, Nancy, 33
lawsuits, 45, 55, 60–62
leafy spurge, 58
Lewing, Mark, 59
Lewis, Meriwether, 16
Liane, Tom, 57
lightning, 13
logging
  to control amount of fuel, 40–41, 66–67
  disease and, 32
  environmental legislation and, 32–33, 36–37
  reinstating fires and, 66, 69
  restrictions on, 18
  salvage, 59–62
  techniques used in, 18, 66–67, 69–70
  uncontrolled expansion of, 17–18
lumbering. *See* logging
Lyford, Gordon, 43–44
Lyford, Nancy, 43–44

Malibu, California, 72
Mileti, Dennis, 55–56
Minor, Kathryn, 53
Minor, Sam, 53

Moore, Michael, 52
Multiple-Use Sustained Yield
  Act (1960), 31

National Environmental Policy
  Act (1969), 31
National Fire Plan, 35–36
National Forest Management
  Act (1976), 31
National Geographic (magazine),
  28
National Interagency Fire
  Center, 38, 42, 50, 75
National Park Service, 9, 28, 38
Native Americans, 13–16
Nature Conservancy, 75
Nelson, Robert H., 27–28, 75
northern spotted owl, 33–34, 35

Oregon Department of Fish and
  Wildlife, 45
O'Toole, Randal, 46–47, 70, 72,
  75
Owens, Bill, 68

Pinchot, Gifford, 25–26, 27, 28
pioneer species, 15
plains, 14–15
plants, 15
politicians, 46, 53, 75
pollution
  Clean Air Act and, 34
  from fire retardant, 44–45
  from smoke, 41, 67
Powell, John Wesley, 16
prescribed burns
  best type of, 76
  Clean Air Act and, 34
  purpose of, 23
  techniques used in, 22
  in wildland-urban interface
    communities, 69–70

public opinion
  after Big Blowup of 1910, 26
  about Bitterroot fires land
    rehabilitation, 60
  about fires as natural events,
    12–13, 18
  about fire suppression, 23, 41
  input process and
    environmental legislation,
    31–32, 36–37
Pyne, Stephen J., 41, 63, 65, 66

railroads, 17
recreation, 35
"Relation of Forests and Forest
  Fires, The" (Pinchot), 28
Resources Planning Act (1974),
  31
Rodgers, Patti, 47, 49
Roosevelt, Theodore, 25, 34

scientific management
  belief in, 25–26, 27–28
  environmental movement and,
    30–31
  firefighting as, 27
  of private industrial forests, 35
Sedjo, Roger, 17, 18, 35
seed germination, 29–30
Sequoia National Park, 28–30
sequoias, giant, 28–30
Shasta-Trinity National Forest
  (California), 33–34
Sheley, Roger, 57
Sholly, Don, 11
Sierra Club, 60
Siskiyou National Forest
  (Oregon), 43–44
Smith, Andy, 46–47
smoke
  as health hazard, 41, 67
  from natural fires, 32

in pre-European America, 14, 16
Smokey Bear, 20–21
soil, hydrophobic, 59
Stahl, Andy, 43
Sula State Forest (Montana), 59–60

Thomas, Jack Ward, 40
Tilford, Greg, 55
Tilford, Mary, 55
timber
  demand for, 17
  fear of lack of, 26
  harvesting
    to control amound of fuel, 40–41, 66–67
    disease and, 32
    environmental legislation and, 32–33, 36–37
    from national forests, 34–35
    reinstating fires and, 66, 69
    restrictions on, 18
  salvage, 59–62
  techniques used in, 18, 66–67, 69–70
  new uses for, 69
  sales from Bitterroot National Forest, 60–62
tourism, 12, 67–68

Umatilla National Forest (Washington and Oregon), 32–33

USDA Forest Service. *See* Forest Service

Varley, John, 12
Verrazano, Giovanni da, 14–15

Wallowa-Whitman National Forest (Washington and Oregon), 32–33
Warner Creek Fire (Oregon), 46
Washington Post (newspaper), 72
weeds, 57–58
Weeks Act (1911), 19
Western Fire Ecology Center, 60
Wilderness Act (1964), 30–31
Wilderness Society, 60
wildfires. *See* fires, natural
wildland-urban interface communities
  Bitterroot Fires and, 52–54, 55
  building codes and, 72–73
  fireproofing measures for, 62, 70–72
  growth of, 41, 55–56
  habitat destruction and, 43–44
  reinstating fires and, 68–69, 70
  responsibility of property owners in, 41, 56, 57, 59, 70, 72
Willamette National Forest (Oregon), 46
Witt, James, 55

Yellowstone National Park, 1988 fire in, 10–12

Picture Credits

Cover photo: © Digital Vision
© AP Wide World Photos, 11, 19, 20, 27, 33, 45, 47, 51, 54, 57, 58, 61, 64, 68, 73
© Snark/Art Resource, NY, 14
Andrea Booher/FEMA, 74
© CORBIS, 29
© Landov, 8, 24, 71
© Photodisc, 42, 67
© UCAR/NCAR/NFS, 40

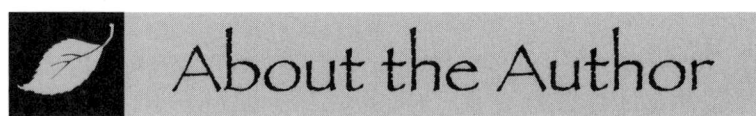

About the Author

Linda E. Platts is an associate editor at PERC, a nonprofit institute located in Bozeman, Montana, and dedicated to improving environmental quality through markets. Her articles have appeared in the *Wall Street Journal* and the *Christian Science Monitor* as well as in regional newspapers and magazines. In addition to editing duties, she writes a newsletter for PERC about grassroots environmental groups. Before joining PERC, she was a feature editor for the *Arizona Daily Star* in Tucson, Arizona. She lives in Bozeman with her husband and two children.